MW01489819

Dunwoody changes lives by building opportunities for graduates to have successful careers, to develop into leaders and entrepreneurs, and to engage in "the better performance of life's duties."

Quote is from the Last Will and Testament of William Hood Dunwoody.

BORN TO DO.

Dunwoody alumni:
stories of impact

Dave Kenney

PUBLISHED BY

Dunwoody College of Technology
Minneapolis, Minnesota

DUNWOODY
COLLEGE OF TECHNOLOGY

Author: Dave Kenney
Design: Blue Hot Creative

ISBN: 979-8-218-48298-5
Libraray of Congress Control Number: 2024917567
First edition: 2024

Printed in the United States of America

This book reflects the recollections of experiences of Dunwoody alumni. Significant effort was put forth to connect with family members for stories in which first-person interviews were not possible. Many were based on previously published materials.

CONTENTS

FOREWORD

Ray Newkirk, 1965

As a business owner, a community member, and an alumnus—I've been a part of the Dunwoody story for nearly sixty years. I've built my own story of success and shared in the stories of colleagues, friends, and acquaintances. And for every story I've heard, there are a hundred more out there. Stories of overcoming challenges, building legacies, and making a difference. They are the stories of people who have left an impact on the industries they work in and the communities they live in.

They are stories worth sharing—about people, companies, and achievements worth remembering.

That belief is what has driven me to help create this book, *Born to Do*, as a way to memorialize just some of the stories that serve as a testament to the Dunwoody Difference.

My own Dunwoody story started at the age of sixteen when I became bound and determined to attend the school as one of the first steps in my manufacturing career. Through the support of my wife, I was able to make that dream a reality.

Dunwoody became the first stop in a long journey that included opening my own Tool & Die shop TAPE Inc. at the age of twenty-three, and then founding, acquiring, and building up numerous other companies during my long career. For me, Dunwoody was the catalyst to my success. It opened doors and created opportunities for which I will be forever grateful.

I've seen Dunwoody be that same catalyst for many others—some of whom are highlighted in this book. From industry trailblazers to community activists, their stories illustrate the importance of technical and skilled trade education. The importance of designing, building, servicing, and creating the products and services that keep our world running.

Like the story of Vern Taaffe, whose work in the field of medical manufacturing has helped improve the lives of those suffering from kidney disease. Or Joel Elftmann, a personal friend, who after getting a degree in Machine Tool would work his way up to becoming an owner and CEO of FSI International, one of the world's leading suppliers of cleaning machines for the computer chip industry. Or the Ferrara family—Ted, Todd, and Claire—who have been improving the quality of life of Minnesota homeowners through their successful family-run business, Standard Heating & Air Conditioning.

I hope that when people read these stories, they see that learning a skill or a trade is something that should be appreciated and valued—and something we should encourage more young people to explore.

For me, these stories aren't just about highlighting the countless leaders and entrepreneurs who are a product of Dunwoody, but about shining a light on how technical education can change lives.

I should know; it changed mine.

INTRODUCTION

Rich Wagner, Ph.D.
President Emeritus
President, Dunwoody College of Technology (2009–2024)

You don't have to look far to see the lasting influence Dunwoody alumni have had on the world around us. Their stories are woven into the fabric of our community—they are stories of innovation, collaboration, and determination.

In my years as President, I've had the privilege of hearing many of these stories firsthand. I've gotten to know the men and women who have used their Dunwoody education to change industries, start companies, and create solutions to complex problems.

Their stories shine a light on the impact Dunwoody College has had and continues to have on the lives of our students and the industries we serve.

I was honored to write the introduction to this new book, *Born to Do*, an idea inspired by a Dunwoody alum to capture the entrepreneurial spirit that is a bedrock of the Dunwoody legacy.

We are proud of all our alumni whose stories serve to inspire the next generation of Dunwoody students. This book highlights some of the accomplishments of our alumni. These stories are a testament to the rigorous hands-on education Dunwoody provides and illustrate the possibilities a Dunwoody education creates. They represent, in the words of our founder, how a Dunwoody education prepares graduates for "the better performance of life's duties."

The success of our graduates brings to light how the Dunwoody story is bigger than what you see inside the walls of our campus. The impact Dunwoody continues to have on students, families, and communities is one of the reasons I was proud to serve this school for nearly three decades.

I love telling the Dunwoody story, and the stories of graduates like the ones highlighted in this book. I hope you will enjoy reading them just as much.

I also know that for every story included in this anthology, there are hundreds more yet to be told. And with every graduating class—hundreds more yet to be written.

FROM THE VERY BEGINNING, IT WAS ALL ABOUT THE DO-ERS

Benefactors William Hood Dunwoody and his wife, Kate, made their fortune in the grain and milling business and were deeply invested in the Twin Cities community. After their deaths in 1914 and 1915, the bulk of their estates, nearly $5 million, was set aside for the establishment of a new post-secondary school in Minneapolis.

Unlike most colleges and universities at the time, the school the Dunwoodys envisioned was to focus on "industrial and mechanical arts." In addition, they wanted the school to offer education "without distinction on account of race, color, or religious practice." William and Kate Dunwoody had discerned a need for a place where young people from all backgrounds could learn "the better performance of life's duties"—to, in the words of a later generation, do the things they were "born to do"—and their bequest was meant to make that vision a reality.

On December 14, 1914, the William Hood Dunwoody Industrial Institute opened in what was known as Old Central High School in downtown Minneapolis with a few dozen students and a curriculum that included classes in machine shop practice, cabinetmaking, millwork, and printing.

In the years that followed, Dunwoody College of Technology has maintained its commitment to technical education and to readying students for what its original benefactors called "life's duties."

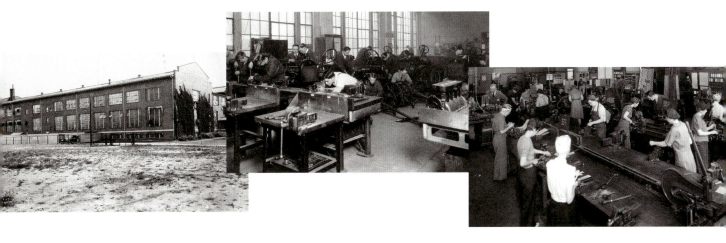

Honoring Milestones

1914–1930

- In 1917, Dunwoody moves from the Old Central High School into two newly constructed shop buildings just west of downtown at its current location.

- In response to World War I, Dunwoody shifts its focus to meet the nation's military needs, training mechanics, radio operators, and bakers for the armed services. By the end of the war, Dunwoody has trained more than six thousand men for military service.

- During the 1920s, Dunwoody adds new programs like building construction, electrical, mechanical drafting, painting, sheet metal, and highway construction. Annual enrollment tops four thousand—about one-third Day School students and the rest employed workers seeking additional Evening School training.

1930–1950

- During World War II, Dunwoody once again answers the call to duty. The school ramps up operations to meet the demand for defense workers, staying open twenty-four hours a day during the week and part-time on weekends.

- Fully half of the four thousand students in the institute's Day School and Evening School enroll in classes preparing them for defense-related occupations.

- Dunwoody introduces short courses in "pre-Army" and "pre-Navy" training, such as the operation and maintenance of military vehicles.

- In response to high demand for workers in defense plants, Dunwoody begins training women for the first time.

- In all, Dunwoody trains about fifteen thousand men and women during the war, almost all of them for war-related work.

- In the years immediately following the war, a majority of the students enrolled at Dunwoody are military veterans.

- Dunwoody's Director, Dr. Charles Prosser, helps pass the Area Vocational Technical School Law, which leads the way to establishing eight technical schools in Minnesota and lays the foundation for technical education in the United States.

- Total annual enrollment holds steady in the 4,200 range.

1950–1970

- In 1965, the school receives a gift from the estate of Henry E. Warren, which includes the property across the street from Dunwoody, on which his Cadillac dealership was located. The school retrofits the building into the new home of its Automotive and Welding departments.

1970–1990

- In 1971, Dunwoody opens its doors to women, a change in policy that leads to the admission of the institute's first post-World War II woman student.

- In 1972, Dunwoody receives accreditation from the National Association of Trade and Technical Schools (NATTS), which makes it possible for students to receive new forms of state and federal financial aid.

- The advent of the personal computer revolution inspires the introduction of new courses in computer-aided design and drafting (CADD) and other tech-focused fields.

- A new commitment to diversifying the student body leads to the establishment of the Youth Career Awareness Program (YCAP), an initiative aimed at improving student retention and graduation rates among students of color.

- In 1989, Dunwoody is named one of ten best technical schools in the United States.

1990–2010

- Dunwoody begins offering bachelor's degrees as well as associate's degrees and certificates.

- In 2002, the school adopts a new name: Dunwoody College of Technology.

- In 2003, Dunwoody merges with NEI College of Technology.

- The first official Dunwoody Alumni Association is formed.

2010–Present

- As Dunwoody maintains its focus on preparing students for high-paying, in-demand careers, it embraces new technologies and expands its curriculum.

- When Dunwoody celebrates its centennial year in 2014, its reputation as a dynamic, fiscally responsible institution is firmly in place.

- Among its new programs are the School of Engineering, the School of Design, and Dunwoody Online, offering multiple online degrees.

- New initiatives like Pathways to Careers (P2C, the successor to YCAP) and Women In Technical Careers (WITC) are created to help foster success among students from underserved and under-represented populations.

- Under President Rich Wagner's leadership, Dunwoody secures the largest gift in its history ($30 million) and completes the two largest campaigns ever ($52.5 million and $75 million).

- In 2023, Dunwoody purchases the Dominion Building to complete its campus footprint.

Today, Dunwoody offers certificates, associate's degrees, and bachelor's degrees in more than forty majors. Hundreds of students graduate each year, ready to enter a diverse, performance-oriented, and modern workforce. They are among the more than 200,000 men and women who have received an education at Dunwoody over the years—alumni who gained the skills they needed to accomplish what they were "born to do."

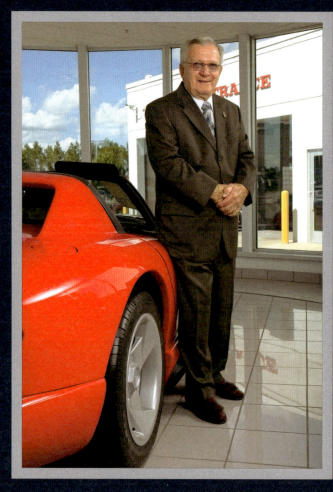

John Adamich

JOHN ADAMICH

Automotive Service Technology, 1954

If you had asked someone during the 1970s to name the most trustworthy journalist in Minnesota, there's a good chance that person would have answered Jim Klobuchar. Klobuchar (the father of future U.S. Senator Amy Klobuchar) was a staffer for the *Minneapolis Star* newspaper, and thousands of Minnesotans read his column every morning to enjoy his wit, storytelling, and—sometimes—sage advice. If Klobuchar chose to write something complementary or laudatory about someone, it was widely seen as an endorsement—especially if that someone ran a business.

Which is why it mattered that Klobuchar's favorite auto dealer was John Adamich.

Klobuchar first encountered Adamich one day in late 1972, when his wife brought her 1969 Mercury Montego, which she said was making a strange noise, into Prestige Mercury in St. Louis Park, where Adamich was general manager. Klobuchar had assured his wife nothing was wrong with the Montego, but she insisted. When the writer called later that day to get an update, Adamich informed him that the car did indeed have a problem: a loose left ball joint. In a column written soon thereafter, Klobuchar admitted he was chastened to learn he had been wrong about the Montego, and a bit annoyed to hear what a good impression Adamich had made on his wife. "He never raised his voice," she told him. "He was very nice and professional and very reassuring."

The Montego experience marked the beginning of a long relationship between Klobuchar and Adamich. In the years that followed, Klobuchar wrote at least eight more columns in which Adamich figured prominently. It was the kind of free publicity that most car dealers could only dream of. Klobuchar's readers learned that Adamich was a man with a "good temper and a long view of humanity's struggles," and perhaps more importantly to a writer who grew up in northern Minnesota, that Adamich was from "the Iron Range, which makes him genetically a man of taste and restraint."

The Iron Range reference was a hint of the car dealer's larger biography. Adamich had grown up in Hibbing, Minnesota, and he moved to Minneapolis during the early 1950s to enroll in Dunwoody Institute's Automotive program. After graduating in 1954, he worked in service, sales, and management at Northside Mercury for fifteen years before switching to Prestige Mercury, where he first met Klobuchar. Then, after about a decade at Prestige, he made his biggest move yet: he and his wife, Betty, invested in the defunct Southside Dodge, at I-35W and Cliff Road, and renamed it Dodge of Burnsville. The dealership grew, and in 1994, they became sole owners. After four decades in the business, Adamich had finally reached the pinnacle of his profession. "I'm in this place [Dodge of Burnsville] seventy-two hours a week," he told Klobuchar. "I love selling cars."

As the years passed, Adamich reinforced his connection with the school where he learned his trade. In 2003, he played a vital role in the establishment of Dunwoody's Chrysler Automotive Program, which trained students to work specifically on Chrysler, Dodge, and Jeep vehicles (now MoparCAP Local). A year later, he joined the school's Alumni Board of Managers. And in 2008, the College dedicated the Adamich Automotive Lab in recognition of his and Betty's many years of support. The auto dealer lauded by his fellow Iron Ranger, Jim Klobuchar, as an "altogether accommodating and civil creature," felt that providing that support was the least he could do. "Dunwoody provided me with the best option—the training I needed to build the skills and work ethic for a lifetime," he said. "It's important for everyone who has been through [its] halls to give back to the College."

Jim Klobuchar

He asks about his new car—weakly

He is an altogether accommodating and civil creature, John Adamich, his occupation notwithstanding.

John Adamich is a car dealer.

Please don't assume any casual slander here. There is no contradiction whatever between being a car dealer and being kind, genteel and a brother to man. I admit these virtues might waver here and there if the prospect displays marks of being a klutz or a marshmallow. In my experience, however, John Adamich has invariably resisted such temptations with good temper and a long view of humanity's struggles. Moreover, he is a native of the Iron Range, which makes him ge-

Buying a new car was a vindication of the faith of our fathers and proof of our credit rating, neither one of which had much value without the other. It was a day and event for which we planned exquisitely and executed on an undiminished high. It began from the moment we strode through irresistible aromas of the showroom and a voice declared—with just the right edge of exuberance to prepare you for your unconditional triumphs ahead—"tell me how I can help you find the car you want and need most."

John Adamich extended his hand.

"Tell me," he said, "how I can help you find the car you want and need most."

John Adamich was columnist Jim Klobuchar's favorite car dealer.

"Dunwoody provided me with the best option— the training I needed to build the skills and work ethic for a lifetime."

—John Adamich

Bunny and Earl Anderson

EARL ANDERSON

Architectural Drafting & Estimating, 1960

Next time you visit one of the roughly 4,500 Walmart stores in the United States, look out for the bollards. Bollards are short, vertical posts, once found mainly in harbors and ports, where they were used to secure the mooring lines of ships and boats. But these days, they're usually installed farther from shore to keep cars and trucks from running into people or structures. Walmart stores, with their sprawling parking lots teeming with moving vehicles and pedestrians, are just the types of places that need bollards to keep everyone safe and reduce the chances of expensive structural damage. During each Walmart's construction, the unheralded vertical posts typically show up in the architectural specifications, under the heading "miscellaneous metals." Someone needs to supply them. And over the years, that someone was more often than not a Dunwoody graduate named Earl Anderson, whose company, Industrial Steel Fabricators, became Walmart's go-to miscellaneous metals supplier.

"They liked us," Anderson said of Walmart's contractors, "so they kept calling us up."

Anderson hadn't planned on making a career in the miscellaneous metals business; it just happened that way. A self-described student of middling abilities, he enrolled in Dunwoody's Architectural Drafting & Estimating program with vague thoughts of designing grocery stores like the ones he had worked at since his teenage years. Dunwoody's placement office initially helped him land a couple of part-time jobs, including one at a company where he was able to do some supermarket design. But then it sent him to one of Minnesota's biggest structural steel fabricators, St. Paul Foundry and Manufacturing. Anderson accepted a full-time position there as a salesman and estimator. His career in metal fabrication was underway.

Earl Anderson's company, Industrial Steel Fabricators, supplied "miscellaneous metals" used at many commercial sites, including Walmart stores.

For more than a decade, Anderson honed his estimating skills on a succession of big construction jobs. During the 1960s, St. Paul Foundry was a major contractor in the building of Minnesota's interstate highway system, and Anderson kept busy figuring out how much the company should charge to supply the structural steel needed for each bridge. Among the other big jobs he worked on were the nuclear power plant in Monticello, Minnesota, and the IDS Center in downtown Minneapolis, where his colleagues occasionally tried to lure him out onto beams, thirty or more stories up, to check out some problem. ("Nope—not going out there!") Eventually though, he yearned to go into business for himself. He bought into a small South Minneapolis company specializing in "light structural steel, stair, and rail fabrication." It was called Industrial Steel Fabricators.

After only a few years with Industrial Steel, Anderson became its sole owner. He strengthened the company's financial position ("I was good with money," he said) and doubled its tiny workforce to eight. Industrial Steel was small, but its reputation was stellar. Emblematic of its work were the jobs it did for Walmart, which included supplying not just bollards but other miscellaneous metals like stairs, lintels, and cart guards as well. "There's over $100,000 of 'junk' in each store that we supply for them," Anderson said.

Many years before, Anderson had received a scholarship to help cover the costs of his Dunwoody education. In retirement, he started making regular financial contributions to his alma mater as a way of showing his appreciation. "Some of my self success was due to luck," he said, "but it was mostly due to the education I received at Dunwoody. I have never forgotten the generous scholarship gift I received, and I hope to pay it forward. I trust Dunwoody to use my gifts where most needed."

"Some of my self success was due to luck, but it was mostly due to the education I received at Dunwoody."

—Earl Anderson

GILROY ARVIG

Electrical Construction & Maintenance, 1953

When Gilroy Arvig took over as president and general manager of what was then known as Pequot Lakes Telephone Company in 1954, he was just twenty-one years old and a recent graduate of Dunwoody's Electrical program. He had returned home to Pequot Lakes after graduation to help out at the company his father had owned since 1919, but figured it was just a short-term proposition. Then his father died. Someone needed to make sure the telephones kept ringing in Pequot Lakes, in Pine River, and at the many farms and cabins dotting the surrounding countryside and lakes area. Arvig accepted the challenge.

At the time Arvig assumed control of the company, rural telephone service was on the brink of a technological revolution. In Pequot Lakes and many other communities in greater Minnesota, people still used candlestick-style phones to place and receive calls through local operators. But in 1955, the newly named Arvig Telephone Company introduced an automatic dial system that let subscribers place local calls directly without relying on an intermediary. It was one of the first independent telephone companies in the State to do so, and it was just getting started.

In the years that followed, Gilroy Arvig demonstrated an avid willingness to embrace technological change. In the 1960s, Arvig Telephone became an early adopter of what was called direct distance dialing, a system that made it possible to make direct long-distance calls using area codes. In the 1970s, it introduced an early mobile telephone service and became one of the first independent companies in the State to let customers buy and install their own phones—including some in colors and shapes that Alexander Graham Bell never could have imagined. In the 1980s, Arvig's parent company jumped at opportunities made possible by the court-ordered breakup of the nationwide monopoly known as AT&T by

Early headquarters of the Arvig Telephone Company.

establishing two new subsidiaries: U.S. Link, one of the first independent long-distance carriers in Minnesota, and a thirty-six-channel cable television system called Interlake CableVision. Finally, in 1994, after forty years at the company's helm, Arvig oversaw its sale to TDS Telecom, a national telecommunications provider. At the time of the deal, Arvig Telecom and its subsidiaries had grown into a company of two hundred employees serving more than forty thousand customers, mostly in central and northern Minnesota.

In a telecommunications landscape that had long been dominated by the monolith AT&T, Arvig stood out as a rare owner who quickly adopted new technologies that only AT&T's regional subsidiaries (including Minnesota-based Northwestern Bell) were initially able to offer their customers.

"He was for sure a pioneer and visionary in the telecom world," his son Greg Arvig said. "He had a lot of first things he did."

Gilroy's grandson Tyler Arvig agreed. "If you were looking for the latest and greatest," he said, "chances are he would have it."

"Thanks to the technical expertise I learned at Dunwoody, I was able to keep up with [telecommunications] industry engineers. I found that I was often as knowledgeable as the engineers, and it was easier for me to learn new technologies."

—Gilroy Arvig

Fresh out of Dunwoody, Gilroy Arvig had moved back to Pequot Lakes thinking he would work for a while at the family telephone business before heading off to do something more directly related to the training he had received in Minneapolis. But as often is the case, circumstances changed. Arvig ended up spending the rest of his professional life in a business quite different from the one he had planned to go into. But that didn't mean he regretted the choices he made about an electrical education. "Thanks to the technical expertise I learned at Dunwoody, I was able to keep up with [telecommunications] industry engineers," he said. "I found that I was often as knowledgeable as the engineers, and it was easier for me to learn new technologies."

Electrical Department class, in the 1950s.

JERRY BECHER

Electrical Construction & Maintenance, 1987

In 1966, Dunwoody Institute embarked on its first major campus expansion since the 1920s. It had recently acquired an adjacent property on the other side of Aldrich Avenue in a bequest from Henry E. Warren, a car dealer who had owned and operated a successful Cadillac franchise on the site for the previous two decades. The property included a large parking lot, which regularly needed to be cleared of snow during the winter. The school contracted with a local rubbish hauler to keep the lot clear. That contractor, in turn, often assigned his teenage son to do the job.

The boy's name was Jerry Becher.

"I can close my eyes and picture plowing snow at Dunwoody," Becher would later recall. "So, I always knew the name."

For many years, that was the extent of Becher's relationship with Dunwoody. His father quit the snow plowing and rubbish hauling business and bought a restaurant in what would later be known as Maple Grove. When his father died a few years later, Becher and his mother took it over and renamed it Mama G's. Becher soon discovered he had a talent for the hospitality business. He renovated the space, improved the menu, and started a hugely popular volleyball league. But his heart wasn't in the work. "Hospitality was a great business," he said. "I liked it. But it was all-encompassing. I didn't want to do it for my whole life." The question was: what *did* he want to do?

As it turned out, Becher had a friend who came into Mama G's periodically to do electrical work. Sometimes Becher helped out. And the more he helped, the more he came to realize that he genuinely enjoyed the work. He decided to become an electrician. But he wasn't the type to jump into anything "half-hearted." He knew that if he were to succeed, he would need solid training. So, in 1986, at the age of thirty-three, he went back to the site of his early snow removal job. He enrolled at Dunwoody.

For the next year and a half, Becher trained to become an electrician along with about twenty other classmates—nearly all of them recent high school graduates. And as he did so, he continued to run Mama G's. Over time, he became friends with one of his Dunwoody instructors, Ron Freeman. After Becher graduated in 1987, he and Freeman started their own residential electrical contracting firm. It was a two-man shop at first: Becher concentrated on the business side while Freeman focused on the field. But as time went by, Becher took on more of the kind of hands-on electrical jobs he had been trained to do at Dunwoody. He and Freeman began hiring new employees, including some recent Dunwoody graduates. The company grew. In 2000, Becher sold a majority of his interest in Mama G's to concentrate more fully on his electrical business, and Freeman retired. Becher brought on a new partner and continued to expand. By the 2020s, J. Becher & Associates had about 150 employees and had added multifamily residential and commercial work to its service portfolio.

Becher was the first to acknowledge that he had gotten into the electrical contracting business by an unconventional and circuitous route. He had known of Dunwoody since he was a teenager, but hadn't thought of attending until he was well past the age of a typical student. By the time he enrolled, he was an experienced businessperson who could have easily continued doing what he was doing. But he knew he wanted something different, and he believed Dunwoody could help. Looking back on the experience, he was sure he had made the right choice. "I took Dunwoody very seriously," he said. "The amount of electrical knowledge I had leaving school was huge. I use it every day."

An Electrical class from the 1980s during the time when Jerry Becher attended.

"I was always the guy that never quit and never stopped. I never thought that failure was an option."

—Jerry Becher

STEVE BRYANT

Electrical Construction & Maintenance, 1968

You know you've become an indispensable employee when the company you work for provides you a house on land it owns—so you'll never be too far away—and then does it again a few years later. This undeniable realization dawned on Steve Bryant while working for West Publishing in the 1980s and 1990s. Bryant had joined West, the Country's foremost publisher of law books, in 1977, less than a decade after completing Dunwoody's Electrical Construction & Maintenance program. He had started with West as an electrical supervisor at its headquarters in St. Paul, but in short order he'd been put in charge of maintaining all the company's facilities, not just its electrical group. Around that time, West decided to build a new manufacturing plant in suburban Eagan, and Bryant started spending more and more time there. That's when West's vice president, John Nasseff, offered to have the company buy an adjacent farm that had recently become available and let Bryant and his family live in an old, brick house that sat on the parcel.

"It needed a lot of renovation," Bryant recalled, "but West paid to have it done."

It also gave him a reserved parking spot outside the main headquarters building—a coveted perk that he had vowed would be his one day.

A few years later, when the company decided to move its entire operation from St. Paul to Eagan, it financed the construction of a new home for Bryant and his family on another part of its sprawling, three-hundred-acre property.

"They wanted me to live very close to the operation," Bryant said.

The unique residential perks Bryant received from West validated an insight he had gleaned years earlier, while training at Dunwoody. It had come by way of an instructor named Jim Swanson. "I wasn't applying myself," Bryant recalled. "He pulled me aside one day and gave me a stern talking-to about wasting opportunity. The crux of his message was, if you apply yourself at Dunwoody, you'll be prepared to take on many other opportunities that you cannot even imagine. And that just stuck with me forever."

The dressing-down from Swanson provided the push Bryant needed to complete his education at Dunwoody, but it was Swanson's more targeted message about future opportunities and the importance of taking advantage of them that made the biggest difference in Bryant's career. After all, Bryant didn't jump straight from Dunwoody into his job at West. He took many steps along the way: aviation electrician with the U.S. Navy; apprentice with the IBEW in California; journeyman electrician back home in Minnesota; master electrician with Blandin Paper Company in Grand Rapids. Each of those steps represented an opportunity recognized and seized.

Even after Bryant and his family moved into their second company-provided home in Eagan, opportunities continued to present themselves. Bryant's work as West's facilities manager brought a promotion to the company's executive suites. Then, when West was sold to Thomson Corporation in 1996, Bryant converted the knowledge he'd gained during the company's relocation and development into new but related business opportunities: starting his own real estate investment company, Bryant Properties, Inc., and acquiring a fifty-percent stake in a contractor that had done most of West's electrical work. In the years that followed, until his retirement in 2015 and beyond, Bryant continued to harken back to the tough lesson he'd learned and internalized from Swanson. "There is no question in my mind," he said. "If this one instructor hadn't pulled me aside and straightened me out, I probably wouldn't have completed Dunwoody, and I seriously doubt things would have turned out as well for me and my family as they did."

"Dunwoody was the springboard for my success and allowed me to take advantage of all the opportunities I was given."

—Steve Bryant

Steve Bryant used the knowledge he gained during his career to start his own real estate investment company, Bryant Properties, Inc.

JOHN CLEVELAND

Automotive Technician Cooperative, 2010

By the spring of 2010, when John Cleveland was finishing up his training in Dunwoody's evening Automotive program, gas-electric hybrid vehicles were well on their way to entering the American mainstream. The Toyota Prius, the world's most popular hybrid, was about to cross the one-million mark in U.S. sales. Unstable gas prices and a new financial stimulus program known colloquially as "Cash for Clunkers" had increased demand for hybrids and other fuel-efficient vehicles. When Cleveland accepted a job offer from Lexus of Wayzata a few months before graduation, the chance to work on hybrids was not at the front of his mind (Lexus, Toyota's luxury brand, had introduced its own hybrid in 2005), but it was definitely a factor. He could see, even then, where the industry was heading.

Over the next four years, Cleveland honed his skills as a technician, first with Lexus of Wayzata, and later with Rudy Luther Toyota. He became familiar with all Lexus and Toyota models, both gas-powered and hybrid. But as time went on, he noticed something unique about the hybrid owners who brought their vehicles into the shop: they almost always assumed they had no choice but to have their cars serviced at the dealership. It was a common misconception. A typical news report from the time asserted that hybrid owners were "pretty much obligated to use the dealer for all of the car's servicing, as no independent mechanic is set up to work on the hybrid's specialized components."

That gave Cleveland an idea.

"I was like, hey, I can do this work," he recalled. "I was already doing it. It was challenging. I was getting better at it. The question I had to ask myself was, 'Why am I doing this for someone else?'"

In the spring of 2014, almost four years after leaving Dunwoody, Cleveland quit his job with the dealership to go into business for himself as an independent mechanic specializing in Toyota, Lexus, and Scion vehicles. In many respects he was honoring a family tradition of entrepreneurship. His grandfather had built a fledgling bank in Minneapolis's Cedar-Riverside neighborhood into one of the nation's most successful small-business lenders. His father had helped turn another local startup, the parts-and-mold manufacturer Protolabs, into one of Minnesota's leading technology firms. Now it was John's turn to try building a business of his own. "It was inevitable," he said. "I didn't know if it was going to work, but I couldn't not do it."

Cleveland's new shop, CARspec, opened the following fall in Eden Prairie, and began marketing itself, as planned, exclusively to Toyota, Lexus, and Scion owners. Business was slow at first. ("Waiting for the phone to ring got really stressful," Cleveland admitted.) But eventually word began to spread among the owners Cleveland was targeting that they didn't need to service their cars at the dealership. By 2020, CARspec, with its staff of two, was accepting new customers only by referral. "It's not hard to keep the two of us busy, which is nice," Cleveland said. "We're very small and plucky. It's easy for me to manage, I enjoy doing it, and it's nice to have the luxury of turning away business every day."

Looking back on the trajectory of his young career, Cleveland couldn't help but smile at what he called his "backwards" path. He had started out by doing what he thought he was supposed to do: he went to a traditional four-year college, the University of Wisconsin–

Madison, and earned an economics degree. From there, he landed a "pretty decent" sales job, but quit after one week. Only after enrolling at Dunwoody did his path forward become clear. "It was so much more practical and so much more applicable to actually being a successful human being and being good at this career," he said. "By going to Dunwoody, I actually learned how to do stuff and fix things and learn how to learn—not to mention how to work really hard when I don't want to."

"By going to Dunwoody, I actually learned how to do stuff and fix things and learn how to learn—not to mention how to work really hard when I don't want to."

—John Cleveland

KENNETH CRONSTROM

Sheet Metal, 1927

Spend enough time rummaging through thrift shops and flea markets—or maybe even your own garage—and there's a decent chance you'll eventually come across an old, aluminum ice chest with a beat-up sticker identifying it as a Cronco cooler. It might even be adorned with a big logo for Pepsi-Cola, 7-Up, or Hamm's Beer. During the 1950s and 1960s, untold numbers of Americans loaded ice-cooled Croncos stuffed with their favorite foods and beverages into wood-paneled station wagons and pull-along camping trailers and hit the road in search of outdoor leisure. Few of them realized that their old, reliable ice chests had a real, if indirect, connection to Dunwoody Institute.

The Cronco cooler was the brainchild of Kenneth Cronstrom, a 1927 graduate of Dunwoody's Sheet Metal program. At the time of his graduation, Cronstrom had no immediate plans to become of manufacturer of consumer goods. Instead, he set out to make a career for himself in a field for which he had been well trained: the fabrication of sheet metal rain gutters and pipes. His company started small, with just three employees, but it eventually grew, adding workers and expanding its services to include the installation and repair of residential heating and air conditioning systems. By the early 1940s, Cronstroms Furnace and Sheet Metal employed twenty-six people and was, in the words of the *Minneapolis Tribune*, "the most modern-equipped firm of its kind in the city."

At some point during the tumultuous years of World War II, Cronstrom began making plans for a postwar pivot. In 1948, his new company, Cronstroms Manufacturing, began operating out of the Hiawatha Avenue building housing his heating and air conditioning firm. Initially, Cronstroms Manufacturing made a variety of aluminum products, including

Cronco cooler for sale at an antique store in Elk River, Minnesota.

office supplies like desk trays and card boxes. But soon it began focusing almost exclusively on its most popular creation, an aluminum ice chest. Advertisements touted the "Deluxe Cronco Cooler" as "the answer to a sportsman's prayer."

> Foods stay FRESH, beverages stay COLD, even on the hottest summer day; hot foods keep their same temperature... in this lightweight aluminum ice chest. Distinctly different.

> Constructed similar to your home refrigerator. Fibre-glas insulation. WATERPROOF, will not leak. Nickel-plated hardware. End drain (with detachable hose) for melted ice. Removable cover, usable as tray. All aluminum, weighs only 15 lbs.

During its first six months of production, Cronstrom's new company manufactured five thousand coolers and began distributing them nationwide. Less than two years later, Cronstrom moved his heating and air conditioning operation to a new location in St. Louis Park, and turned the Hiawatha building into a facility dedicated exclusively to manufacturing. The company gained traction. It started making coolers for the retail giant Montgomery Ward, and signed agreements to produce branded versions for breweries and soft drink makers around the Country. The *Minneapolis Tribune* reported that a national publication specializing in reviews of consumer products rated the Cronco cooler "easily the best box tested." In 1958, the company churned out 260,000 Croncos.

By the 1960s, Cronstrom's dominance of the portable cooler market was beginning to wane. The Coleman Company had recently acquired the patent for a rival Styrofoam-insulated design, and its new, lightweight plastic coolers were proving to be very popular. Cronstrom responded by introducing new products such as metal food storage carts used in hospitals and aluminum doors and window frames that resisted frost and condensation. The Cronco cooler became a historical relic.

Kenneth Cronstrom died in 1985 at the age of seventy-eight, but his manufacturing and HVAC companies lived on. They continue to operate today under new names and ownership. If you search for him in the historical record, you'll find only infrequent mentions of his accomplishments, but you may still get a sense of his commitment to the school that helped make them possible. For many years, Cronstrom remained an active member of the Dunwoody Alumni Association and served on the school's Alumni Board of Managers. Keep that in mind if you should ever happen across an old, banged-up cooler with the Cronco logo still visible on the front.

"What started out as a small sideline of portable ice coolers has become a nationwide business for Cronstroms Manufacturing."

—*Minneapolis Tribune*, July 29, 1955

Sheet Metal department, 1948

HARVEY DAHL

Electrical Construction & Maintenance, 1961

When Harvey Dahl graduated from high school in the farming community of Rosholt, South Dakota, in 1958 (ranked eighteenth out of eighteen students, as he would later recall), he thought he had everything figured out. He'd marry his high school sweetheart, Joyce Wickander, spend the summer working for a local electrician, and in the fall, start training to become a schoolteacher at Northern State Teachers College (NSTC) in Aberdeen. And everything worked out almost exactly as he planned—except for the teacher thing. "They told me, 'You're better off doing something else,'" he recalled of his instructors at NSTC. "I asked them, 'What do you want me to do?' They said, 'Get a job and see what you can do with it.'"

Dahl figured he would just return to work with the electrician who had hired him over the summer, but when he got back to Rosholt, the man told him there wasn't enough work to go around. Dahl was in a bind. He had enjoyed working with the electrician and was starting to think he might like to become one himself. When he asked his former boss for advice on how best to enter the field, the electrician suggested he enroll for electrical training at one of two schools: North Dakota State School of Science in Wahpeton, or Dunwoody Institute in Minneapolis. Dahl didn't have to think twice about which one to choose. "I knew where Wahpeton was, and I didn't want to go up there," Dahl said. "Joyce and I packed up everything we had in a trailer and drove to Minneapolis."

Dahl got into Dunwoody, bought a slide rule, punched his timecard, and got to work. "I didn't fool around much," he said. "I was there to learn." To get by financially, he brought home loaves of bread from Dunwoody's Baking program and worked full-time as the school's maintenance man. "It was kind of an easy, nice job," he recalled. "I enjoyed it."

Electrician jobs were scarce in the Twin Cities area when Dahl graduated in the spring of 1961, so it took several months before he could join the union and become an apprentice. But once he landed his first job, he was almost always gainfully employed. Every six months, the union sent him to a different shop, and at each stop, he picked up new skills. After about ten years of working for other people, he decided to venture out on his own. In 1973, he and Joyce started Medina Electric in the basement of their home. Two years later, they moved it into an old barn in nearby Loretto.

Initially, Dahl took whatever work he could get. His first job as Medina's only electrician called on him to wire a friend's new home. "I had never wired a house in my life," he later admitted. "The inspector said, 'Harvey, you've got enough wire in there for four houses.'" It didn't take long for Dahl to realize that residential work wasn't for him. He hired another electrician friend to work on houses so that he could focus exclusively on the kind of commercial and industrial jobs that did not, in his words, require him to "deal with homeowners." As time went on and demands on his time grew, he hired more and more electricians, and started concentrating on the business side of the operation—the estimating, bidding, and buying of materials.

In the nearly thirty years that Harvey and Joyce Dahl owned Medina Electric, the company grew from a one-electrician shop into a thriving business with about seventy-five employees. And while hard work and good business sense were probably responsible for the bulk of their success, Harvey didn't hesitate to give at least part of the credit to his alma mater. "There's no school better in this world than Dunwoody," he said. "I would have never, ever been anyplace without it."

"There's no school better in this world than Dunwoody. I would have never, ever been anyplace without it."

—Harvey Dahl

Harvey and Joyce Dahl with their Medina Electric partner, Roger Georges (left).

JAZMINE "JAZ" DARDEN

Engineering Drafting & Design, 2017

In the summer of 2015, Dunwoody beefed up its Robotics & Manufacturing department with the addition of three new 3D printers provided by Stratasys, a global leader in the developing field of additive manufacturing. That same summer, an educator and budding entrepreneur named Jazmine "Jaz" Darden visited Dunwoody on a whim and asked for a campus tour. Darden had driven past Dunwoody daily on her way to and from her job with Minneapolis Public Schools, where she led Girls in Engineering, Mathematics, and Science (GEMS) and Guys in Science and Engineering (GISE) programming, and she was curious to find out what went on behind the College's brick walls. During her tour, she found plenty to intrigue her, but the things that really piqued her interest were the 3D printers. It dawned on her that, with 3D printing, she might be able to turn some of the ideas that were always bouncing around in her head into actual gadgets and products.

"I was like, this is fascinating," she recalled. "I thought, where do I sign up?"

From the day Darden enrolled at Dunwoody, she was among the most unconventional students to ever attend the College. She had grown up in nearby Brooklyn Park, and was, like many Dunwoody students, a hands-on tinkerer who excelled in science and math. But other elements of her biography were less typical. For one thing, she already held four-year bachelor's degrees in both physics and mathematics from Augsburg College. For another, she had two years under her belt as a full-time employee with Minneapolis Public Schools. And then there was the fact that she was a Black woman—or, as she put it, "the only girl and only student of color in my classes." Her non-traditional background was on full display her first day of class. "I had my hair down," she recalled. "Nice shirt, shorts, pair of Sperrys. I walked into machine shop class and, as I remember it, my teacher was like, don't ever show up like that again. ... So that night I went home, got some work boots, jeans, and black T-shirts, and that's what I wore to school every day."

Jazmine "Jaz" Darden works with students during a SPARKZ3D camp on the Dunwoody campus.

Over the next two years, Darden learned everything she could about design and manufacturing. After graduating in 2017 with a degree in Engineering Drafting & Design, she continued to nurture her fascination. She learned how to build her own 3D printers and assembled a small army of them, which she eventually put to work creating new products, including the I AM EarHero™, an adjustable band for face masks used during the COVID-19 pandemic. In the meantime, she learned that Dunwoody was introducing a new program of night classes focused exclusively on 3D printing. When she expressed interest in enrolling, her former instructors urged her instead to come back as an adjunct faculty member. She agreed. In the years that followed, she taught dozens of students who shared her fascination with 3D printing. "I almost feel like I'm a team lead," she said. "I'm learning along with them."

Darden continued to cultivate her entrepreneurial instincts even as she taught at Dunwoody. Among other things, she established SPARKZ3D, an organization focused on delivering hands-on science, technology, engineering, and math (STEM) programming with an emphasis on 3D printing. In the spring of 2023, SPARKZ3D held its first fully funded 3D printing camp for Minneapolis Public School students at Dunwoody. With her in-depth knowledge of 3D design and printing, Darden was carving out a niche for herself as a maker of things who enjoyed passing along what she knew. "I love inspiring other people and teaching them about this technology that's right at our fingertips," she said. "I'm grateful I can do it, but it's rewarding when I can teach them how to do it for themselves."

Darden strengthened her bond with Dunwoody by serving on the college's Alumni Association Board and by delivering the keynote address at its 2022 commencement. Off campus, she served on the Works Museum Board of Directors, the NASA's Minnesota Space Grant Consortium Advisory Board, and the MINNDEPENDENT STEM Advisory Committee, and was named a "Women in Business Honoree" by *Minneapolis/St. Paul Business Journal*. She also earned accolades as a skilled public speaker with an inspiring message: "Live to the level of your smile." In 2024, she became a full-time applications engineer with GoEngineer, a reseller of computer-aided design (CAD) software and additive manufacturing equipment.

"I love inspiring other people and teaching them about this technology that's right at our fingertips. I'm grateful I can do it, but it's rewarding when I can teach them how to do it for themselves."

—Jazmine "Jaz" Darden

PAUL DAVIS

Refrigeration, 1979

By the time Paul Davis became a journeyman pipe fitter in the mid-1980s, a quiet technological revolution was just starting to get underway, one that would have major implications in his chosen field of refrigeration. With the advent of client-server computing, businesses and organizations were setting up facilities known as "data centers" to house their computers and networking equipment. The dense concentrations of servers inside those new facilities generated a lot of heat that had to be mitigated, and that mitigation couldn't be achieved without custom refrigeration systems. This situation created a new demand for mechanical contractors capable of doing the type of piping and service capabilities required to keep data centers cool. It was what Davis would later call a "niche."

Davis first learned the importance of developing specialties when he went to work as a journeyman at a St. Paul mechanical contracting firm co-owned by his father (himself a Dunwoody graduate) and a partner. "They were already in a niche market, doing specialized piping systems and service for other mechanicals and industrials," Davis recalled. "I learned from them how important it was to do what they were doing, to do it well, and to build a strong network of customers and contacts in the industry."

In 1995, after the prolonged illness and death of his father, Davis teamed up with a friend to start a new company, Bloomington-based Whelan-Davis, which took to heart the concept of finding niches. While his partner specialized in piping ultra-pure water systems for medical device manufacturers, Davis focused on two other areas of expertise: upgrading school heating and cooling systems (mostly summer work) and installing and maintaining refrigeration systems for those data centers, full of heat-emitting servers, that were popping up all over the Twin Cities area. "It was a developing market," he said. "Early on we were doing a lot of work for companies like Dayton's and Target. They were growing and growing and growing, and we grew with them. We also worked with multiple phone companies and manufacturers."

Two decades after graduating from Dunwoody, Davis had achieved a level of success he had never imagined possible. "Those first five, ten years after my partner and I joined together were the most rewarding," he said. "It was a blast. We were defying the odds that said most small businesses crash and burn in less than five years." At its peak, Whelan-Davis employed about two dozen people. When Davis's partner retired in 2008 and Davis bought him out, the company shed its process plumbing operations and focused primarily on the specialty areas Davis had developed over the years. Newly named Davis Mechanical Systems halved its workforce while continuing to do the things it did best. It was a reflection of Davis's business philosophy: to find a niche and stick to it. "There are a lot of companies in the Twin Cities that are more general in nature," he said. "They try to do a little bit of everything and do all their work in-house. But that's not always the most efficient, most cost-effective way to do it. Sometimes you may not have the expertise or the licensing in-house to get the work done quickly. In our case, we had the experience and talented technicians to get the cooling systems built on time, and on budget."

Davis sold his company in 2018, and stepped away from the trade in which both he and his father had made their livings. Looking back on his career, he credited his Dunwoody education with helping to make it all possible. "I got such excellent training that I felt I had an edge in the industry," he said. "Dunwoody does an excellent job of training people in what's applicable, what's up to date."

Paul Davis developed a niche market installing and maintaining refrigeration systems for data centers.

"I got such excellent training that I felt I had an edge in the industry. Dunwoody does an excellent job of training people in what's applicable, what's up to date."

—Paul Davis

Don Dolan with Dunwoody President Frank Starke.

DON DOLAN

Electrical Construction & Maintenance, 1964

On Thanksgiving night 1982, a fire broke out in the sixteen-story home of Northwestern National Bank (one of William Hood Dunwoody's enduring business ventures) facing Marquette Avenue. More than one hundred firefighters responded to the call, but they couldn't save the building. The fire caused at least $75 million in damage, which made it one of the costliest disasters in the City's history. It also left hundreds of bank employees with no place to work, and forced Northwestern (a predecessor of the current Wells Fargo) to activate an emergency relocation plan. The bank started making urgent calls to contractors capable of converting available real estate into temporary offices. Among the people who received those calls was Don Dolan, the president of a middling electrical contracting firm called Parsons Electric. Dolan and Parsons had recently lost a bid on another job for Northwestern, but had made a good impression in the process. The head of the bank's properties division asked Dolan if Parsons—which at the time had only about a half dozen electricians—could handle all the electrical work that would need to be done to put Northwestern's displaced employees back to work. Dolan told him it could.

In the weeks that followed, he made sure it did.

"That was my first bit of success with Parsons," he later recalled.

Still, it wasn't clear at the time Dolan made his promise to Northwestern Bank that he or his company would be able to follow through. After all, his path to that moment had been somewhat indirect. He had gotten involved in electrical contracting almost by accident two decades earlier, when he enrolled at Dunwoody Institute with only a vague idea of what he wanted to study. During his second year there, an instructor convinced him to switch his focus from electrical fieldwork to management. After graduating from Dunwoody, Dolan went to work at a small Twin Cities electrical contractor, Hoffmann Electric, and started a long climb to the top of the company's management ladder. Fourteen years later, he was fired from Hoffmann after attempting to make changes the owner objected to. At that point, Dolan was seen by some in the business as damaged goods, and it was not clear where he might end up. But in 1978, he bought into Parsons Electric, a respected but somewhat limited local firm that did maintenance and service work and not much else. He was still struggling to build up the company four years later, when Northwestern Bank chose him and Parsons to help it relocate its employees after the Thanksgiving fire.

After that, Parsons grew at a phenomenal pace. By the time Dolan sold the company in 1998, it had expanded from a firm with a handful of electricians and less than $1 million in annual revenue into one of the Twin Cities' most successful electrical contractors, with more than five hundred employees and sales topping $52 million annually. In the years that followed, he would look on with pride as his successors turned the company he transformed into an even larger regional and national powerhouse.

Dolan had started his career in electrical contracting by enrolling at Dunwoody in 1962 without any clear idea of what he wanted to do. In fact, he had chosen to enter the school's Electrical program mainly because he had a distant family member who was a self-taught electrician, and he figured if his relative could do electrical work, he could, too. But the real turning point had come one year into his training, when a faculty member urged him to think of himself as management material. Many years later, when asked whether he was glad he had taken his instructor's advice, he couldn't help but laugh.

"It was a tremendous decision," he said.

Don Dolan and Parsons Electric helped Northwestern Bank recover from its devastating fire in 1982.

"My Dunwoody instructor, John Tillsbury, told me, 'Maybe you don't want to become an electrician. Maybe you want to work inside as a project manager.' So that's what I did. They changed my curriculum. I had less lab work and less wiring, but more academia."

—Don Dolan

JOEL ELFTMANN

Machine Tool Technology, 1960

Joel Elftmann, by his own admission, was never a "particularly great student," but by the same token, he never thought of himself as "not being smart," either. He was a worker. Throughout junior high and high school in South Minneapolis, he held a series of jobs—newspaper carrier, grocery store clerk, hotel fry cook—and he assumed he would just keep working, perhaps in the trades. By the time he graduated, he had landed yet another job, an entry-level position at a Minneapolis plastics manufacturer called Booker & Wallestad, and he had an eye on its toolroom. He enrolled in Dunwoody's Machine Tool program, kept his job at Booker & Wallestad, and eventually parlayed his first year of training into an apprentice toolmaker position with the company. When he finished at Dunwoody in 1960, he had a full-time job waiting for him there.

"I was a good mold maker," he said.

At that point, Elftmann had no reason to think that his budding career would eventually veer off into the world of high technology. But Booker & Wallestad had begun doing custom tooling and molding for companies like General Electric, Bell Labs, and Texas Instruments, whose manufacturing requirements were growing increasingly complex. The worlds of old-school manufacturing and newfangled technology were colliding. In 1966, Elftmann joined his boss, Vic Wallestad, at a spinoff company, Fluoroware, that custom fabricated parts for the electronics industry. Among the products Fluoroware made were Teflon carriers, or "boats," that held silicon wafers used in the manufacture of early semiconductors. And it was during a visit to one of Fluoroware's clients that Elftmann had a bright idea. He noticed that the wafers held by Fluoroware's boats went through a cleaning process that required a worker to dry them by hand. It was an "aha" moment. "I thought, why don't I just make a machine that spins that thing?" he recalled.

The local press closely followed Joel Elftmann's career over the years.

Elftmann was about to take his first big step into the world of high tech.

In 1973, Elftmann and Wallestad spun off another company, this time from Fluoroware. The new firm, FSI International, based in Chaska, started by developing Elftmann's "spin dryer" mechanism for semiconductor manufacturing, and then grew from there. It expanded its product line to include spray and vapor-based systems for cleaning, etching, and decontaminating microchips, a photolithography process that defined circuit patterns on chips, and a system that controlled the flow of chemicals in the manufacture of semiconductors. As microchips got smaller and more complex, Elftmann made investments in technology and people to keep up with changing demands. He also made a big investment in himself by completing a three-year program in smaller company management at Harvard University—a course of study that, in his words, "cleaned off the rough edges" of a toolmaker looking to make good as a corporate executive in the high-tech world. By 1988, he was the CEO of one of the world's leading suppliers of cleaning machines for the growing computer chip industry, a company with total sales of about $45 million and a workforce of 350.

Along the way, Elftmann grew accustomed—sort of—to the wild gyrations of the computer chip industry. During upswings, FSI went gangbusters as it raced to fill orders for its clients. But when the industry hit one of its frequent downturns, the company had to cope with loss of revenue while continuing to maintain its technological edge through investments in research and development. Longtime FSI board member Jim Bernards marveled that a person with Elftmann's background could make sense of it all. "I don't know that a toolmaker from Dunwoody could break into the business [today] and make such a mark like Joel has," he said. When Elftmann finally stepped down as CEO in 2000, FSI was back on top with annual sales of more than $200 million and nearly seven hundred employees worldwide, and he was ready for a break. "I've been through eight of these cycles through my career," he said. "They wear you out after a time."

In retirement, Elftmann turned his attention to other pursuits, including a deeper involvement with his alma mater. He served on the College's Board of Trustees, including a stint as chair, for more than two decades. In 2006, he and his wife, Mary Ann, provided funding for Dunwoody's new Elftmann Student Success Center, a tutoring and academic support hub for students needing extra help in skill development. When asked why he made the donation, Elftmann insisted it was his way of showing thanks for the scholarship he received to attend Dunwoody many years before. "I need to pay back, to invest in new students," he said. "Somebody invested in me."

"You come to Dunwoody and you learn a skill, you use that skill, get employed, and then through your course of employment, you go to different levels."

—Joel Elftmann

JACK ELMER

Baking, 1960

For nearly four decades, residents of Portland, Oregon—especially those with a fondness for sweets—have been finding their way to a little shop on the southeast end of downtown called JaCiva's. When it first opened in 1986, JaCiva's was something of a pioneer, a locally owned and operated purveyor of handmade gourmet chocolates and pastries. Its name was a mashup of the first names of its husband-and-wife proprietors, the Elmers. Iva Elmer kept the place running during good times and bad. Jack Elmer was the creative force behind most of the shop's sugary confections.

Jack had received his first formal training many years earlier at Dunwoody Institute.

It almost seemed as if Jack Elmer was destined to be a maker of sweet things. As the story went, his mother instilled in him a love of baking when he was a young boy growing up on his family's farm, east of Portland. At age ten, he was baking cakes for friends and family. After graduating from high school in the late 1950s, he traveled more than 1,700 miles away from home to enroll in the Baking program at Dunwoody. Two years later, he had the training he needed to start a career in the field he loved.

Elmer returned to the West Coast and opened a bakery in Gresham, Oregon, not far from where he had grown up, but he had to supplement his income by working on the side at a couple of commercial bakeries. A few years after that, he made what he would later describe as a life-altering visit to a "European-styled" pastry shop. Inspired by what he saw there, he traveled with his young family to Switzerland, where he trained to become a "konditor," a high-end pastry chef. After returning to Oregon, he put his newly earned expertise to work at a new venture, Heidi's Swiss Pastries, located in a small village of

Scene from the Dunwoody Baking program that Jack Elmer completed in 1960.

Alpine-themed businesses on the road to Mount Hood. Over the next fifteen years, he built Heidi's into one of the top retail bakeries on the West Coast and burnished his reputation as a uniquely talented pastry chef.

Eventually, though, his talents grew to include a different type of confection: chocolates. With his second wife, Iva, at his side, he went to work honing a new skill. "We were like little mad scientists in the basement," Iva recalled. "We'd come up with all these formulas and different centers and things like that." After selling sweet treats out of their basement for about a year, they opened their new shop, JaCiva's Bakery and Chocolatier, in Southeast Portland in 1986.

In the years that followed, JaCiva's became known almost as much for being a community asset as it was for being a purveyor of sweets. Customers came to expect warm hugs from Jack whenever they visited the store. They shook their heads in admiration at the way he cared for patrons and employees, especially during difficult times. "He was very personal, and he touched people's lives," said Laura Boscole, Iva's daughter, who took over the family business in 2012. "When someone would come in, they weren't just a customer, they were instantly a friend or family."

Jack had his own struggles along the way. In 1990, he suffered a near-fatal stroke that made it difficult to even squeeze a pastry bag, but after a long recovery, he returned to the shop, doing what he did best. Ten years after the stroke, he was diagnosed with prostate cancer. He died in 2014.

Jack Elmer did not leave behind any final thoughts about his education at Dunwoody or about the role it played in developing his life's passion. But in 1961, a year after he graduated, he shared some insights with the school's quarterly alumni publication. He had recently started his first business, the bakery in Gresham. His successes as a pastry chef and chocolatier were still to come. But he recognized even then that his time in Minneapolis was crucial. When asked how he rated his Dunwoody experience, his answer was unequivocal: "Excellent," he said. "[I] would never have my bakery now without it."

When asked how he rated his Dunwoody experience, Elmer's answer was unequivocal: "Excellent," he said. "[I] would never have my bakery now without it."

Paul Englund

PAUL ENGLUND

Machine Tool Technology, 1958

It's a lucky man who gets to combine his job with his passion.

Paul Englund was a lucky man.

Englund was a tool and die maker. He learned his trade while attending Dunwoody Institute in the late 1950s. After earning his diploma, he went on to establish his career in the usual way, taking jobs at local companies like the Hopkins-based injection molding firm Thermotech. Eventually, he ventured out on his own, organized an independent union of local toolmakers, and opened his own tool-and-die shop. But he apparently was never completely satisfied with the path his career had taken. Something was missing. So, at the age of fifty, he retired and started putting his skills to work in a way that allowed him to focus more on his favorite pastime: duck hunting.

He became a maker of duck calls.

Englund's interest in hunting and waterfowl dated back to the 1940s, when he made his first trip to Lake Christina, near Alexandria, one of Minnesota's most famous duck-hunting spots. His father was a cook at a duck camp there, and through that connection, Englund was able to watch as wealthy hunters bagged their limits of "cans" (canvasbacks) and redheads. One day, while monitoring the action from a blind, he picked up a spent shell, put it to his nose, and inhaled. "From that moment on [I was] obsessed with waterfowling," he said.

Englund's waterfowl obsession existed separately from his work during all his years as a tool and die maker, but once he retired, he was free to merge the two. "We had a second garage," his daughter, Jill, recalled. "It was filled with snowmobiles, motocross bikes, and God knows what else. One day I went out there to find he had transformed it into a tool shop. There was a lathe, exotic woods, and all sorts of equipment. It was like, wow, okay, Dad you are off and running." In his new shop, the "Dr. Quack Shack," Englund started turning out duck and goose calls—some of them finely crafted from exotic woods like cocobolo, Osage orange, and kingwood; others made of new-age plastics, using techniques he mastered in the tool-and-die trade. He called his little business Paul's Calls.

Englund worked at his own pace. A wood call took him a couple hours to make; a plastic one, a little more than that. He could turn out about 125 of them each year. His reputation grew—first locally, then nationally. A few of his designs, like the Pit Boss goose call, became collectors' items. As demand for his calls grew, Englund faced a decision: should he keep Paul's Calls a one-man operation, or should he expand it into something larger? He had discovered during his years as a tool and die man that he didn't particularly enjoy being a boss. Working on his own seemed to suit him. When a national retailer of outdoor goods proposed to carry his calls if he would ramp up production, he declined the offer. "I make as many calls as I want," he said. "I don't need any more business."

Englund had found a way to merge the skills he first learned at Dunwoody with his lifelong love of hunting and the outdoors. And in the process, he had made a name for himself as one of the nation's premier call makers. But the satisfaction he got from his late-blooming success could only approximate the thrill he experienced each time he fooled a mallard with one of his calls. That, he believed, took just as much skill as turning a call on a lathe. "If you want to be a good caller, you're going to have to work at it," he said. "You've got to practice. Duck calls are like musical instruments. You're not going to buy a violin Friday and play Carnegie Hall on Sunday."

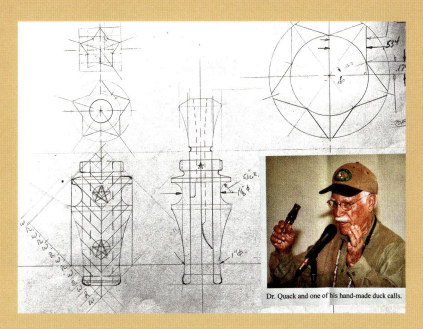

Dr. Quack and one of his hand-made duck calls.

Specifications for one of Paul Englund's calls.

"Duck calls are like musical instruments. You're not going to buy a violin Friday and play Carnegie Hall on Sunday."

—Paul Englund

Late 1940s Baking program, around the time the

ROBERT, CHARLES, AND WILLIAM ENTENMANN

Baking, 1949, 1949, and 1950

They're some of the most recognizable grocery items in the United States—pastries encased in blue and white boxes with cellophane windows, all emblazoned with a single name: Entenmann's. For more than a century, the company founded in 1898 by German immigrant William Entenmann has been churning out cakes, doughnuts, muffins, and cookies by the millions. But it hasn't always been a national brand. During its first few decades, Entenmann's was a relatively small operation, based in the Bay Shore community of New York's Long Island, a bakery that delivered many of its products door-to-door. It wasn't until the early 1950s that the company started to set its sights higher. And by then, it was under the leadership of William Entenmann's three grandsons, Robert, Charles, and William III—all of them alumni of Dunwoody's Baking program.

The Entenmann brothers attended Dunwoody in two shifts: Robert and Charles in 1949, and William in 1950. At the time, the Entenmann bakeries were being run by their father, William Jr. But a year after the brothers completed their Dunwoody education, William Jr. died, leaving them and their mother, Martha, in charge. Not long after, the company began to change. Entenmann's phased out door-to-door delivery and shifted its focus exclusively to wholesale. It stopped baking breads to concentrate on its sweeter product lines. And in 1961, it moved into a new, much larger production facility in Bay Shore—one that would expand several times during the coming years. Its increasingly passionate fan base included singer and actor Frank Sinatra, who kept a standing order for crumb cake. By the late 1960s, Entenmann's distribution area stretched from southern New Jersey to Springfield, Massachusetts, and encompassed the entire New York metro region.

The three brothers, with their Dunwoody training, split the company's management duties. Robert was the salesman. Charles had a flair for engineering and administration, and oversaw automation of the cake lines. William was the baker, the one who sampled products before they shipped. And there was a lot to sample. In 1969, the company's weekly ingredient list totaled nearly one million eggs, 12,000 pounds of butter, almost 200,000 pounds of flour, 5,000 pounds of hazelnuts, and 3,500 pounds of cocoa. A few years later, it introduced what would become two of its bestsellers—a chocolate chip cookie and a chocolate-dipped doughnut—and opened a new production plant in Miami, Florida.

When a reporter with *New York Newsday* interviewed Charles about the company's success, the middle brother revealed a family secret: he wasn't a big fan of sweets. "I probably eat more cake from our competitors than I do of our own products," he said. "We test, we eat!"

By 1976, Entenmann's employed more than two thousand people at its bakery complexes in Bay Shore and Miami. The brothers took the company public, and in 1978 sold it to a pharmaceutical company, Warner-Lambert, for $233 million. Entenmann's changed hands a few more times after that, and in 2002 was acquired by its current owner, Bimbo Bakeries USA, one of the Country's largest commercial bakers.

In the years following the sale, Robert, Charles, William, and other members of the Entenmann family honored the brothers' Dunwoody connection with financial support of the school. In 2012, during a visit with Dunwoody President Rich Wagner, Charles Entenmann reminisced about his time in Minnesota. He told Wagner he was especially grateful to his Dunwoody baking instructor for expanding his knowledge of the ingredients used in cakes. He also offered some sage advice for any student on the cusp of a technical career. "Mind your own business and do your job better than the other [person]," he said. "Someday, [they'll] be working for you."

"Mind your own business and do your job better than the other [person]. Someday, [they'll] be working for you."

—Charles Entenmann

Baking students show off their creations in 1949, when the Entenmann brothers attended.

Dick Ericson (right) and Minneapolis Millers
General Manager George Brophy check the turf at the new
Metropolitan Stadium, 1959.

DICK ERICSON

Air Conditioning, 1958

In the days leading up to the Minnesota Twins' first World Series appearance in 1965, Dick Ericson, the head groundskeeper at the Twins' home ballpark, Metropolitan Stadium in Bloomington, made it clear that he and his crew intended to "play it fair." The Twins' World Series opponents, the Los Angeles Dodgers, were known for their speed on the bases, and rumor had it that the Twins might try to slow them down by spreading extra sand on the base paths. But Ericson promised there would be "no gimmicks like that" at his stadium. That's how his boss, Twins manager Sam Mele, wanted it, he said. That's how it would be.

For a couple games, at least.

The Twins won the first two games of the series, at the Met, without resorting to any groundskeeping shenanigans. But then they lost the next three games in Los Angeles, where the Dodgers and their speedy shortstop, Maury Wills, took full advantage of their home field's hard-packed base paths. Down three games to two, the Twins decided they could no longer afford to let their opponents steal bases at will. Ericson received new instructions.

> When they came back here again, they wanted to counteract [the Dodgers' speed]. What did we do? We went to first base and we took a wheelbarrow of sand—we dumped it right out there, so when Maury Wills got ready to run, he was in loose sand. It would be like if you've ever run on the beach, it's hard to run, see? And that's how you can alter your field. If it's too loose, it's going to be slow. And if it's hard, it's going to be fast for the runners.

The Twins won game six, but then lost the final game and the series, despite the additional sand. Ericson's attempt to slow down Maury Wills became a mostly forgotten episode in Twins history, but his efforts on behalf of the ballclub cemented his reputation as a team player and helped him build a long career in professional sports.

One other little-known fact about Ericson? He was Dunwoody graduate.

Ericson had enrolled at Dunwoody during the early 1950s, when he already had several years of groundskeeping experience. He had gotten his start at Lexington Park, home of the minor league St. Paul Saints, and had since moved across the river to Nicollet Park, where the Minneapolis Millers played. His position at Nicollet Park was seasonal, so he may have decided it would be in his best interest to get training in a field besides turf management. Although he started taking classes in Dunwoody's Air Conditioning program during the off-season, his in-season baseball duties frequently interrupted his training, and he ended up taking four years to complete his degree.

By then, though, it was becoming clear to Ericson that the second career path he had chosen might not be necessary. During his years as a Dunwoody student, he had risen to become head grounds supervisor at Nicollet Park, and had then moved over in the same capacity to the new Metropolitan Stadium, the construction of which was instrumental in convincing Major League Baseball and the National Football League to expand into Minnesota.

For three decades, Ericson worked to keep the home playing surfaces in top game-day condition for the Twins, the Minnesota Vikings, and, from 1976 to 1981, the Minnesota Kicks of the North American Soccer League. For most of that time, he plied his trade at Met Stadium. But when the Twins

and Vikings moved to the new Hubert H. Humphrey Metrodome in downtown Minneapolis in 1982, Ericson joined them. And it was there, in Minnesota's first indoor stadium, that he finally got to put his knowledge of heating, refrigeration, and air flow to full use. On game days, he was the one who made the call on whether to turn on the air conditioning as the lights went on and thousands of fans (each one giving off the heat of a hundred-watt bulb) streamed in. If the forecast called for snow, he decided how much heat would be needed to melt it off the stadium's inflated roof. Dunwoody hadn't trained Ericson to perform those specific tasks, but that didn't matter. It hadn't taught him how to slow down a speedy baserunner by adding a little extra sand, either.

"Dick's my idol. He is a terrific groundskeeper. He can do it all. In the old Metropolitan Stadium, he always had the field in good shape despite the cold."

—George Toma, fellow NFL groundskeeper

MARK FALCONER

Welding, 1968

One day a few decades ago—it was probably the 1990s—a local sales representative for a centuries-old Irish beer walked into the offices of Mark Falconer's Minneapolis Oxygen (MO2) looking for help. The company that owned Guinness was launching a big push to put its beer on tap in bars and restaurants around the Country, including the Twin Cities, and its plan depended on finding dependable local sources of the particular mix of gases that gave draft Guinness its signature creamy head. After meeting first with MO2's sales manager, the Guinness rep asked Falconer and his plant manager whether they could mix nitrogen and carbon dioxide.

"Yeah," they said. "You tell us the percentages, and we'll do it."

In no time at all, Guinness lovers throughout the Twin Cities were downing fresh pints of their favorite stout thanks in part to the efforts of Minneapolis Oxygen.

The story of MO2's contribution to what turned out to be an impressive jump in local Guinness consumption ranked as a minor highlight in the company's current seventy-five-year run as a supplier of industrial gases and welding supplies. But it was also a good example of how Falconer, the man largely responsible for the company's success, relied on expertise to grow his business. He may not have had much experience supplying product to the hospitality industry when the Guinness rep approached MO2, but he knew gases and how customers used them. It was a level of expertise he traced back to his training as a welder at Dunwoody Institute. "Dunwoody gave me a good understanding of how gas and welding products are utilized in manufacturing, in construction, repair, whatever the case may be," he said. "The more you can understand about the product, the better off you are because you can help your customer and develop your relationship."

Falconer had enrolled at Dunwoody during the mid-1960s, after a childhood spent in and around the welding supply business. His father, a Minneapolis Oxygen employee, had bought the company a few years earlier, and encouraged his son to train in welding at Dunwoody so he could come back to MO2 with a better understanding of its customers' needs. So, that's what Falconer did. By the time he finished the program in 1968, he had the technical knowledge he needed to convince customers he knew what he was talking about. "The processes I learned at Dunwoody made me a more well-rounded individual," he said. "It gave me an understanding of why we sell this product, why we sell that product."

After graduating from Dunwoody, Falconer enrolled at the University of Minnesota with plans to study business, but he left after three semesters to work full-time for MO2. He started at the bottom, driving trucks, delivering gas cylinders, waiting on customers. But he eventually moved up, first into sales, and then into management. In 1983, he succeeded his father as president. In the years that followed, he oversaw a major shift in focus. For most of its history, MO2 had been primarily a distributor of oxygen and acetylene, the gases most commonly used in welding and cutting. But by the 1980s, demand was growing for three other gases it supplied: argon and carbon dioxide for plasma and laser cutting; and nitrogen for food processing and packaging. Over time, MO2 started focusing more and more on those products. In other words, it honed its expertise to meet its customers' needs.

And that, in a nutshell, is how Falconer and his team at MO2 were able to so easily supply the unique mix of gases that were needed to make draft Guinness widely available in the Twin Cities. But it was just one example. MO2's established expertise was an equally important factor in becoming a gas supplier to other clients like food processers, health care providers, and research laboratories. Looking back, Falconer couldn't help but wonder at the turns his career had taken since his days at Dunwoody. And he credited his training there with giving him the foundation he needed to successfully adapt. "You go to school for one or two years, but you never stop learning," he said. "You never stop moving forward within your industry, because if you do, you're going to be left out in the cold."

"You go to school for one or two years, but you never stop learning. You never stop moving forward within your industry, because if you do, you're going to be left out in the cold."

—Mark Falconer

Todd, Ted, and Claire Ferrara (left to right)

TED, TODD, AND CLAIRE FERRARA

**Refrigeration, 1977; Sheet Metal, 1980;
Heating & Air Conditioning Systems Design, 2011**

When Tony Ferrara started a heating company in his parents' Northeast Minneapolis home in 1930, he had no formal training and no plans to get any. It was the start of the Great Depression, and supporting his family took precedence over pursuing an education. But in the end, it didn't really matter. His company, Standard Heating (later known as Standard Heating & Air Conditioning), did remarkably well during the 1930s, despite the poor economy. After a few years in business, Ferrara moved his growing firm to more spacious facilities in Dinkytown. In 1941, he relocated it again, this time to a two-story building on Lake Street that, in his estimation, provided "ample room to display the large selection of furnaces, oil burners, gas conversion burners, [and] stokers that we have always considered necessary to successfully conduct a heating and air conditioning business." Ferrara had turned himself into a successful businessman without ever going to school to train in his chosen field.

And yet he understood more than most people the value of a technical education.

Ferrara had nine children, and two of them—sons Ted and Todd—expressed interest in working for Standard Heating once they were old enough. Tony Ferrara urged them both to go to Dunwoody.

"My father was a big advocate for Dunwoody," Ted recalled. "Many of our installation personnel and repair personnel had received their educations there, and he was familiar with the programs and the people who ran them. So even though he himself hadn't gone to school there, he knew enough and was a real believer in how Dunwoody could change people's lives."

Claire Ferrara served as committee chair of the Kate Dunwoody Society, which raises scholarship dollars for women attending Dunwoody.

Todd echoed his brother's assessment. "Our father was ahead of his time," he said. "He knew that education and skill, technical skill, was going to help us elevate our ability to understand the business, understand the people, understand the products that we were delivering into people's homes."

Ted graduated from Dunwoody's Refrigeration program in 1977. Todd completed the school's Sheet Metal program three years later. Both of them went straight to work for Standard Heating, with Ted gravitating toward the service side of the business and Todd focusing on the construction side. In 1981, Tony Ferrara retired, handing the reins of his half-century-old firm to his sons. Ted took over as president. Todd became vice president. In the years that followed, Standard Heating & Air Conditioning grew into one of the region's most successful HVAC companies.

But the story of Standard Heating and its connection to Dunwoody did not end there. In 2006, Ted's daughter, Claire, spent the summer between semesters at St. Catherine University toiling in the company's installation department, and discovered she loved the work. "I liked how all those parts of the puzzle fit together to help somebody be comfortable in their home," she said. Three years later, while she was still finishing up her bachelor's degree in sociology at St. Kate's, she enrolled at Dunwoody, just as her father and uncle had. "I had been exposed to the school from when I was young," she said. "I knew it was kind of the gold standard of technical training."

"My father was a big advocate for Dunwoody. … Even though he himself hadn't gone to school there, he knew enough and was a real believer in how Dunwoody could change people's lives."

—Ted Ferrara

After graduating in 2011, with a degree in Heating & Air Conditioning Systems Design, Claire went to work for several years for a couple larger employers. In 2016, she returned to the family business as a sales representative. And then, three years later, after demonstrating to the family that she was ready, she acquired majority ownership from her father and took over as president of the company.

Standard Heating & Air was now a third-generation enterprise.

Tony Ferrara had started the company during the Great Depression with no special training, but he believed his sons would be better prepared to carry on his work if they received a Dunwoody education. Those sons—and, as it turned out, one granddaughter—came to agree with him on that.

As Ted saw it, Dunwoody was a positive force. "It changes lives," he said. "As you learn more, your interest grows. It multiplies. And that's what Dunwoody is. It's kind of a force multiplier for education."

To Todd, it was a perfect fit. "It was an excellent decision for me to go there," he said, "because I'm more of a doer, more of tactical guy than a strategic guy."

And for Claire, it was the educational boost she needed to successfully run a business. "It was almost like my MBA," she said. "It was the two years that really set me on my career trajectory."

TOM GAUTHIER

Machine Tool Technology, 1966

Tom Gauthier was still in high school in the late 1950s when he first went to work in the shipping department of Rochester Products, a company owned by his father, Emil Gauthier. The firm was a little over a decade old at that point, and had become quite successful making medical devices based on designs developed at Rochester's Mayo Clinic. Among the company's most promising products was a flexible, easy-to-use IV catheter that could be inserted into a patient's vein while causing a minimum of discomfort and allowing maximum freedom of movement. It was known as the Rochester Plastic Needle. When Gauthier first started working in Rochester Products' shipping department, he packed up and sent out maybe a few dozen needles each day. But as time went on, he found it harder and harder to keep up with the orders. By the mid-1960s, the Rochester Plastic Needle was establishing itself as an indispensable tool of the medical trade, and Gauthier was witness to its growing success. Under his father's direction, total unit production would eventually climb above three million.

But Gauthier had no desire to work indefinitely in his father's shipping department. After graduating from high school in 1962, he enrolled at a local technical college with dreams of becoming an engineer. Then he had a change of heart. "I decided I didn't really want to be an engineer," he recalled. "I liked working with my hands better than sitting at a desk." He had gotten some limited experience working in his father's machine shop, and had enjoyed the work. He decided he wanted to be a machinist or toolmaker. A few months after finishing his pre-engineering courses, he started taking classes at Dunwoody.

"It was the greatest," he said. "I learned a whole lot about life—and toolmaking, too."

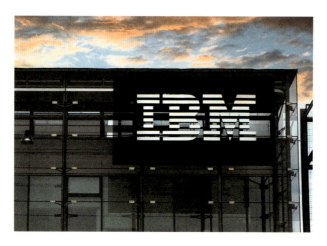

Rochester Medical Equipment, known today as Gauthier Industries, supplied components to companies like IBM, General Electric, and Rockwell Collins.

When Gauthier graduated from the school's Machine Tool Technology program in 1966, he had several good job offers waiting for him from Twin Cities employers, but Rochester was calling him back. By then, his father had sold the rights to the Rochester Plastic Needle to the pharmaceutical giant Johnson & Johnson, and had started a new manufacturing business in his company's old facility. He was also nearing retirement. Gauthier returned to Rochester, intent on putting his new Dunwoody-developed skills to work, and on guiding his father's company in new directions, including metal stamping and precision metal fabricating.

The company, now known as Rochester Medical Equipment, had by that time started doing work for another of the City's biggest employers—IBM. IBM was just beginning to evolve from a midsize manufacturer of tabulating equipment and typewriters into the world's largest computer company, and it relied on smaller firms, like Rochester Medical Equipment, to supply many of its machines' vital components. "My forte was being able to look at a manufacturing process and come up with better ideas of how to do it that would save the customer time and money," Gauthier said. "I did that for a lot of different companies." Over time, the Gauthiers' client list grew to include other high-tech firms, including Zero-Max Industries, General Electric, ITT Aerospace, and Rockwell Collins.

Gauthier took over from his father and kept Rochester Medical Equipment on its new course. In 1978, the firm was nearly destroyed in a flood that damaged or destroyed all of its inventory and equipment. In 1984, Gauthier gave the company a new name—Gauthier Industries—and moved it to a new and much larger facility, where it is still located. Until his retirement in 1997, he continued to run his company with a commitment to business flexibility, a trait he insisted he picked up during his years at Dunwoody. "It gave me the freedom to make choices in my life and career," he said of his training in machining and toolmaking. "My Dunwoody instructors taught me to critique my own work and always strive for the best—skills that have been keys to my success."

"My Dunwoody instructors taught me to critique my own work and always strive for the best—skills that have been keys to my success."

—Tom Gauthier

Wayne Glanton (center) at a construction site with businessman Wheelock Whitney (far left), publisher Cecil Newman, and brother John Glanton (far right).

WAYNE GLANTON

Architectural Drafting & Estimating, 1946

William Hood Dunwoody had endowed the school that bore his name with a directive clearly stating that its programs be offered "without distinction on account of race, color, or religious practice." But in fact, during its first few decades of operation, Dunwoody Institute enrolled few students of color. One of the first to attend was a member of the class of 1946, a World War II veteran named Wayne Glanton. "I never saw any other Blacks around there," Glanton would recall years later. "Sometimes I thought maybe I was [the first one] because some of the teachers would come up and shake my hand and say, 'Glad you're here!'"

Glanton grew up in South Minneapolis, attended Central High School, and enrolled in the Construction program at Dunwoody after graduating in 1941. But his studies were interrupted by World War II. He was drafted into the Army Air Corps, sent to Fort Belvoir, Virginia, for training as a typographic draftsman, and served in Europe. After his discharge, he returned to Minneapolis to finish his schooling at Dunwoody. During his final semester, he was chosen to be one of four students (the other three were white) to represent the school's Architectural Drafting program at the Northwest Builders Home and Garden Show at the Minneapolis Auditorium.

Once his training at Dunwoody was complete, Glanton entered a labor market that was notoriously inhospitable to African Americans. Many employers refused to hire Black workers, and the trade unions weren't much better. (A 1945 survey conducted by the Governor's Interracial Commission found that Black workers accounted for only one percent of union membership in Minnesota.) With so many doors closed to him, Glanton felt fortunate to land a position as a drafting engineer with Hennepin County. It was a job he would hold for more than twenty years.

Wayne Glanton started advertising in the Black-owned *Minnesota Spokesman-Recorder* during the early 1950s.

Glanton's position with the County brought him into regular contact with many Minneapolis power brokers—including Mayor and future U.S. Vice President Hubert Humphrey—and he was not shy about pressing some of his well-placed friends and acquaintances for help in improving living and working conditions in the African American community. In 1968, he and his brother John (another former Dunwoody student) formed Glanton Construction Company with the expressed intention of encouraging young Black people to enter building trade apprenticeship programs, and helping Black craftsmen become qualified subcontractors. As time went on, Glanton often partnered with white contractors and overwhelmingly white unions that were struggling to meet new affirmative action hiring requirements.

Glanton Construction specialized in building simple but functional structures, both residential and commercial. It was among the local firms that built houses for Wausau Homes. It also financed and constructed one of the most iconic buildings in Minneapolis's African American community: the Fourth Avenue South headquarters of the *Minnesota Spokesman-Recorder* newspaper, maybe the oldest continually operating Black-owned business in Minnesota history. Like most Glanton projects, the *Spokesman-Recorder* building was unpretentious, the opposite of monumental. But unlike many flashier buildings, it went on to gain special distinction as an officially designated historic landmark.

In 1984, Glanton became the first Black Dunwoody graduate to be recognized with an Alumni Achievement Award. In announcing the honor, President Warren Phillips cited Glanton's many contributions to the community, and to the school, where he continued to volunteer as an advisor to a new generation of students. It was a fitting recognition for a man who had spent his life overcoming obstacles and laying foundations—both literal and figurative—that helped other people of color succeed. Decades earlier, while Glanton was still attending Dunwoody, the Black-owned *Spokesman-Recorder* had run a short feature reporting that his instructors believed he had "a very excellent future in his chosen field." Those Dunwoody instructors turned out to be more prescient than they ever could have imagined.

Glanton received an Alumni Achievement Award in 1984, a fitting recognition for a man who had spent his life overcoming obstacles and laying foundations—both literal and figurative—that helped other people of color succeed.

Mike Hanson at the grill during a barbeque lunch at Hunt Electric.

MIKE HANSON

Electrical Construction & Maintenance, 1985

Over the years, plenty of Dunwoody graduates have gone on to earn additional degrees at other institutions of higher learning. Less common are those who've enrolled at Dunwoody with four-year diplomas already in hand. And among that cadre of atypical Dunwoody students, even fewer ever arrived holding a bachelor's degree in history—with minors in English and political science.

That non-traditional student's name is Mike Hanson.

Hanson grew up in southwest Minneapolis and graduated from high school in 1977, with few, if any, thoughts of entering the trades. He wanted to become a lawyer, so he enrolled at the University of Minnesota, and over the next four years, he dabbled in a couple of academic disciplines before settling on history. After graduation, he applied to several law schools and was accepted by three of them. But then he calculated how much each would cost and the additional debt load he would have to assume if he wanted to attend. Law school started to lose its appeal.

Hanson was familiar with the trades. His grandfather was a sheet metal foreman. His father ran the construction division of a local contractor, Sterling Electric. His brother was an electrician. And Hanson himself had worked as a temporary journeyman wireman at his dad's firm while he was attending the U. Once it became clear that law school was financially out of the question, his father suggested he switch course and pursue a career in the trades at Dunwoody. So, that's what he did. He enrolled in Dunwoody's Electrical Construction & Maintenance program, and paid for his classes by working part-time. The history major with law school dreams was on a completely new career path. "I didn't necessarily think I was going to be an electrician," he said, "but if that was the path I was going down, so be it. I was twenty-five years old, I'd been living on my own for six years, and I had to pay bills. My brother had made a good career for himself as an electrician. I thought, okay, that's what I'm going to do."

It turned out to be a good decision. Upon graduation from Dunwoody in 1985, Hanson landed a job at Hunt Electric with the understanding that he would work his way up into a project manager role over the next three years. Ultimately, it took less than a year for his bosses to entrust him with a project he would run on his own. Throughout the rest of the 1980s and early 1990s, Hanson continued to advance through Hunt's management ranks. In 1993, he enrolled in the executive MBA program at the U of M's Carlson School of Management. Three years later, not long after receiving his MBA, he became Hunt Electric's president. In his subsequent twenty-five years at the helm, Hanson helped turn Hunt into one of the biggest electrical contractors in the United States, with annual revenues growing from $35 million when he took over in 1996 to $535 million on his retirement in 2021.

Hanson had enrolled at Dunwoody and embarked on a career in the trades after concluding that law school was unaffordable. Even then, he wasn't sure he wanted to be a field electrician. But he quickly learned that, at Dunwoody, there wasn't just one path for him to take. "The nice thing about Dunwoody was they taught the underlying theory really well," he said. "For me, in the Electrical program, that was the difference. If you have the aspiration to be the crew leader, to be the general foreman, to run the project, to start your own company, Dunwoody's the place for you. It'll give you the skills you need."

Mike Hanson gets ready to tackle one of his many presidential responsibilities: the judging of Hunt's annual ugly sweater contest.

"For me, in the Electrical program, that was the difference. If you have the aspiration to be the crew leader, to be the general foreman, to run the project, to start your own company, Dunwoody's the place for you. It'll give you the skills you need."

—Mike Hanson

Electrical department, 1918

CHARLES HENTSCHELL

Electrical Construction & Maintenance, 1917

Charles Hentschell spent his entire career in the newspaper business, but he was never a journalist. His one foray into the world of reporting came early in his career when he moonlighted as the golf editor of the *Minneapolis Tribune*. And even then, his attempts at journalism were not what one would call hard-hitting. His account of one golfer's encounter with a helpful rodent was typical of his style:

> Miss Josephine Taylor [is] thinking seriously of adding trained gophers to [her] golfing paraphernalia as a result of observing one of the pests at the Minneapolis Golf Club.

> On the tenth hole, Miss Taylor's ball in the rough was obligingly removed to a nice lie in the fairway by a gopher, who seemed well-versed in Chesterfieldian requirements.

As Hentschell's short and relatively undistinguished stint on the sports page suggested, his interest in newspapers lay elsewhere—on the production and business sides. He had landed his first job as a teenager in the *Tribune*'s production department, loading reels of paper onto printing presses. But he considered the position a dead-end proposition, and a short time after starting at the newspaper, he enrolled in the Electrical program at Dunwoody Institute, hoping to improve his prospects. Upon graduation in 1917, the *Tribune* hired him as an in-house electrician. From there, Hentschell started a slow but steady climb up the job ladder—including his brief detour into sports writing—that culminated with his promotion to mechanical superintendent. In 1935, he accepted a similar position with the *Tribune*'s crosstown rival, the *St. Paul Dispatch* and *Pioneer Press*. Not long after that, he was named production manager.

The *St. Louis Post Dispatch* was one of the nation's top newspapers during Charles Hentschell's tenure there.

Hentschell was doing well for himself, but he still had plenty of rungs left to climb.

In 1940, the *St. Louis Post-Dispatch*—at the time, one of the nation's most respected newspapers—was looking to expand its capabilities by adding a production annex to its St. Louis headquarters. It hired Hentschell to oversee the project, and provided him with yet another opportunity to continue ascending the corporate ladder. The *Post-Dispatch*'s publishers—initially Joseph Pulitzer II, and then his son, Joseph Pulitzer III—took an immediate liking to their new hire, and started entrusting him with greater and greater responsibilities. They promoted him to business manager of the *Post-Dispatch* and later general manager of the paper's parent company, Pulitzer Publishing. They put him on the company's board of directors and on the trust that administered the Pulitzer family's vast fortune. By the 1950s, Hentschell was essentially the second-most powerful executive at one of the most successful publishing companies in the United States.

Hentschell's importance to the Pulitzers was evident in the many business deals they entrusted him with over the years. One of them, the 1951 acquisition of a rival newspaper, the *St. Louis Star-Times*, was a good example. The Pulitzers put Hentschell in charge of the negotiations, but they expected him to keep them informed at every step along the way. At the same time, they wanted to make certain that other potential bidders didn't find out what they were up to. So, they devised a code based on fruits and vegetables, and instructed Hentschell to use it in his communications with them. When the *Star-Times* owners opened the negotiations with an asking price of $6.25 million, Hentschell picked up a pencil and went into secret agent mode. "It took me an hour to write that damn thing," he recalled many years later. "You can imagine trying to decipher $6.25 million into melon, squash, pickles, and Christ knows what else."

Hentschell's education at Dunwoody hadn't directly prepared him for a high-flying corporate career that, on at least one occasion, called on him to use vegetable-based cryptography, but through it all, he maintained a fondness for the school. Even in his final years before retirement, when he became publisher of the Pulitzers' (Tucson) *Arizona Daily Star*, he kept his Dunwoody diploma on display. "He thought enough of that thing to frame it," his son, Jim, remembered. "Dad was very proud of his Dunwoody degree."

"He thought enough of [his Dunwoody diploma] to frame it. Dad was very proud of his Dunwoody degree."

—Jim Hentschell on his father, Charles Hentschell

EDGAR HETTEEN

Reappearance Reconditioning of Automobiles, 1939

As a kid growing up on a farm in the far northwestern corner of Minnesota, Edgar Hetteen didn't put much stock in book learning. On the last day of eighth grade, in the spring of 1935, he declared himself done with school. "I was ready for the world," he later recalled. That summer, at the age of fourteen, Hetteen landed his first real job at his uncle's shop, the OK Machine Company, in the nearby town of Roseau. At first, he did mostly odd jobs— tidying up, scrubbing floors, keeping the woodstove filled—but with time, his uncle and his uncle's partner started trusting him with more meaningful work. He learned about welding, machining, and metal shaping. For several years, he stayed at OK, absorbing as much as he could about the business. But by 1939, he was itching to try something else. One day, he walked across the alley to a Chevrolet garage and asked for a job. The owner knew Hetteen from his work at OK, but the owner didn't need any more mechanics. So, he made the eighteen-year-old an offer. He'd give Hetteen a job as an auto body repairman, under one condition: he'd have to take a course in bodywork at Dunwoody Institute. Hetteen didn't hesitate.

"I loaded up my old car and drove down to Minneapolis," he said.

Hetteen took only one course—"Reappearance Reconditioning of Automobiles"—during his short academic career at Dunwoody, but it was enough to show he was serious about making something of himself. With his Dunwoody certificate in hand, he returned to Roseau to start his new career fixing wrecks and rollovers. But when World War II came, and customers stopped worrying so much about how their vehicles looked, his boss put him on cars that needed work under the hood. He became a mechanic.

When the war ended, Hetteen opened his own one-man shop, Hetteen Hoist & Derrick, and set out to manufacture and market a new apparatus that he had thought up—a rig designed to plant wooden telephone poles into the ground. With more business than he could handle on his own, he hired two employees: his younger brother, Allan, and a longtime friend named David Johnson. Together, the three young men turned Hetteen Hoist & Derrick into an uncommonly innovative shop known for manufacturing inventive contraptions such as weed sprayers, garbage can stands, and straw choppers. They changed the company's name to Polaris, and kept expanding their product line.

In late 1955, while Edgar Hetteen was away on vacation, David Johnson cobbled together a machine that would change their lives and launch a new industry. Inspired by a brochure for a "motor toboggan" designed by Wisconsin inventor Carl Eliason, Johnson built his snow-going machine from a pile of seemingly random parts—among them, a nine-horsepower Briggs & Stratton engine, a grain elevator track studded with welded cleats (for propulsion), and a salvaged Chevrolet bumper (for skiing over snow). When Hetteen returned from vacation and learned what his friend had been up to, he was miffed. "Why was David wasting his time like this?" he asked himself. "Our factory builds farm equipment."

But Hetteen soon changed his mind. Within a year, Polaris was gearing up to mass-produce what it now called the Sno-Traveler. The company built up a network of sales reps and dealers. By 1960, snowmobiles accounted for about a quarter of its gross sales. But all was not well. After leading a successful proof-of-concept expedition to Alaska in March of that year, Hetteen returned to Roseau to discover that two skeptical members of Polaris's board of directors remained unconvinced of the snowmobile's potential. Hetteen left the company in a huff. His brother Allan took over. A year later, Edgar founded a new company

Edgar Hetteen (center) with Allan Hetteen and David Johnson, 1948.

in Thief River Falls, about seventy miles southwest of Roseau, and started manufacturing snowmobiles. He called his new snow machine Arctic Cat. For many years after that, Edgar Hetteen's Arctic Enterprises and Allan Hetteen's Polaris Industries engaged in an intense but friendly rivalry that helped spur the development of the snowmobile industry—and later, the development of another innovation, the all-terrain vehicle.

In the years that followed, Edgar Hetteen started several other businesses and proved himself to be a serial entrepreneur whose restlessness harked back to that day in the fall of 1939 when he showed up at Dunwoody, intent on bettering himself. "There is always a better way if you want to look for it," he said. As one of snowmobiling's innovators, he knew what he was talking about.

"There is always a better way if you want to look for it."

—Edgar Hetteen

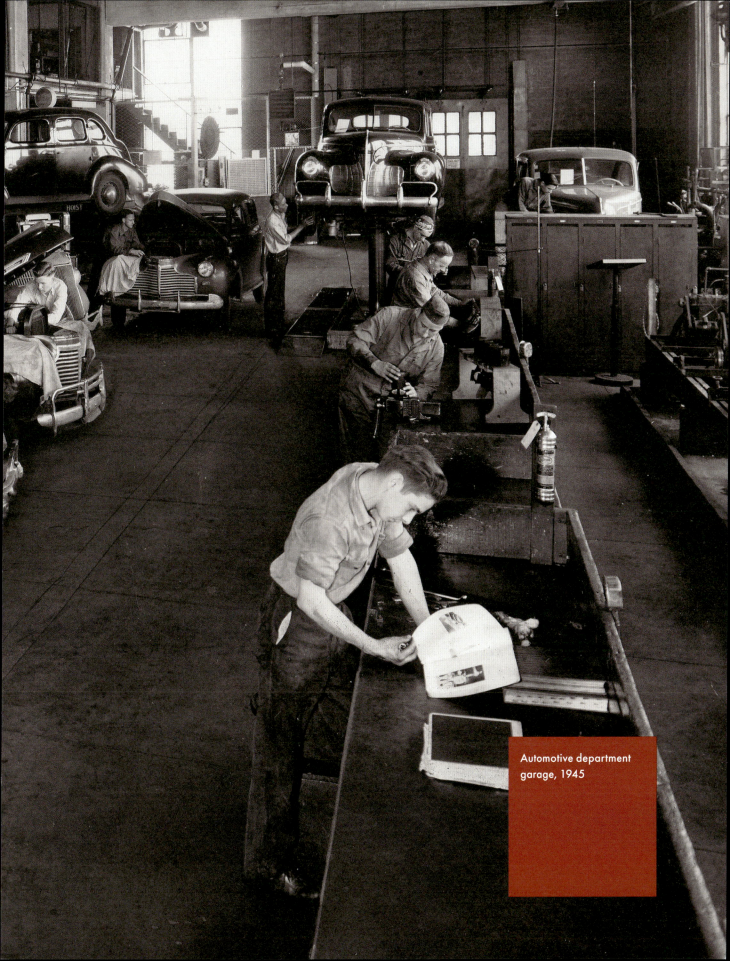

Automotive department garage, 1945

CATHY HEYING

Automotive Service Technology, 2010

Cathy Heying enrolled in Dunwoody's Automotive Service Technology program in the fall of 2008, as what was known at the time as a "non-traditional" student: female; thirty-eight years old; an established career in social services focused on housing and homelessness; no experience as a mechanic; and no particular interest in cars. On one of her first days of class, instructor Dave Duval asked her and her classmates to face a display of crankshafts. "I had no idea what a crankshaft was," she later recalled. "So, I was like, where's everybody else looking? Okay, I'll look there." A few weeks into the program, she was ready to drop out. "We were trying to flare brake lines, and I could not get it," she said. "By the end of it, I was feeling stupid because I was the 'girl' who was crying." After class, Heying told Duval she wanted to quit. Years later, she could still recite his response almost word for word.

> This burly, grumpy guy said, "You're not going to quit. You are smart and you can do this and you've got a great vision and I am going to help you get through not only this class, but any class you need help with in your two years at Dunwoody. You come back and I will help you and I will support you and I'm going to watch you walk across that stage to get your diploma in two years." He was true to his word.

Heying stuck with the program and graduated in 2010, thanks in large part to the personal support she received from Duval. But for those who weren't familiar with her story, a big question remained: Why? Why give up an established career in the social-service field, and then take out student loans to spend two years learning a new trade?

For Heying, the answer to that question lay in her many years of experience helping people in need. Over and over again, she had encountered clients whose lives were in danger of being thrown into chaos by the loss of reliable transportation. Some needed a working automobile to get to and from work. Others needed to prove they had access to a car to qualify for jobs. Still others depended on their vehicles for shelter. Heying saw a gaping need for affordable car repair, and she set out to do something about it.

Three years after graduating from Dunwoody, Heying opened the Lift Garage in a vacant bay at a car wash in South Minneapolis. Unlike most garages, it was set up to operate as a nonprofit, with grants and donations covering the bulk of each customer's repair costs. Demand for the Lift's services quickly outstripped Heying's ability to supply them. The garage's waiting list grew longer and longer. Initially open only on Saturdays, the Lift added days to its schedule and expanded from one bay to four. Heying started hiring paid technicians to take over for the volunteers on whom she originally depended. In 2018, the Lift moved to a new five-bay facility at Lake Street and Hiawatha Avenue. Where Heying once was happy to fix four cars a month, now she was overseeing an operation that handled closer to 140. And still, the waiting list grew.

During the Lift's first ten years in business, Heying helped hundreds of people in need get their cars back on the road at a cost they could afford. There were plenty of less happy outcomes, too—of cars too expensive to fix or vehicles too far gone to ever be driven safely again—but in almost every case, Heying insisted she felt honored to "be part of somebody's story." And she knew she probably never would have had a chance to participate in those stories if she hadn't gone back to school. "I am so grateful I landed at Dunwoody," she said. "For somebody like me, it was like, oh my God, this is so helpful to start with the real basics. It was the right place for me."

"I am so grateful I landed at Dunwoody. For somebody like me, it was like, oh my God, this is so helpful to start with the real basics. It was the right place for me."

—Cathy Heying

Minneapolis Mayor Jacob Frey proclaimed April 13, 2023, The Lift Garage Day.

C. W. HINCK

PRESENTS HIS

THRILL DAY ATTRACTIONS

FOR FAIRS AND CELEBRATIONS

GENERAL OFFICES
830 HENNEPIN AVENUE
MINNEAPOLIS, MINNESOTA

THE ORIGINAL
CONGRESS OF THRILLERS
A COMPLETE PROGRAM
FOR LARGE FAIRS

FRANK WINKLEY'S
SUICIDE CLUB
PRESENTS A THRILL DAY
FOR SMALLER FAIRS

CONTINUOUS OPERATION SINCE 1919
MOTORCYCLE RACES - AUTO POLO - AIR EXHIBITIONS - AUTO RACES
HEAD ON COLLISIONS - SENSATIONAL STUNTS OF ALL KINDS

C. W. Hinck's many thrill show ventures included
a partnership with a well-known auto and motorcycle
daredevil, Frank Winkley.

C. W. HINCK

Aviation Mechanics, 1918

The five thousand or so people gathered at the Seymour, Wisconsin, fairgrounds on the last Sunday of summer, 1925, craned their necks to watch the spectacle playing out in the sky above them. A biplane was buzzing in their direction at an altitude of about a thousand feet. On one wing stood a man, apparently oblivious to dangers most people took for granted. As the plane approached the grandstand, the daredevil leapt into the air. Many spectators gasped. A few screamed. After several seconds, a parachute burst open from directly below the plane. (It had been hidden from view in a grain sack.) The falling man took hold of two cords and started manipulating his descent. When he finally landed, feet-first, on an open patch of grass not far from the grandstand, the crowd erupted in applause. Nearby, a heavyset man named Clarence Hinck smiled to himself with satisfaction. His crew had pulled off another death-defying stunt. And no one had died. Thank goodness.

C. W., as Hinck liked to be known, was a showman, one of the most successful aerial impresarios of the early twentieth century. His flying circus, Federated Fliers, crossed the Country, putting on thrill shows at county and state fairs. In addition to wing walking and parachuting, his band of aeronautical showoffs performed a host of other breathtaking feats, including tight, three-plane "battle" formations, tailspins, and an especially tricky maneuver that called on a stuntman to climb from a speeding automobile to a flying plane on the rungs of a dangling rope ladder. "You had to make sure you didn't get down so low that the ladder hooked on the exhaust pipe or the back bumper," Hinck said. "Guys got killed that way."

Hinck didn't do much flying himself. He considered himself a promoter, not a pilot. But he knew aviation. During World War I, he had enlisted in the U.S. Navy and trained to become a machinist's mate.

He did his training at Dunwoody Institute.

Hinck was one of several hundred cadets who learned their trade at Dunwoody's short-lived "naval school." Established soon after the United States entered the war in 1917, the school specialized in training aviation mechanics. By the time Hinck graduated in 1918, the war was almost over, and he suspected he would never serve in active duty. He started making plans to put his training to new, peacetime uses.

In 1919, Hinck partnered with the school's former commandant, Lt. Commander Colby Dodge, to form Federated Fliers, Inc., a Twin Cities–based aviation company offering instruction, aerial photography, and pleasure flights to paying customers. The company started with eighteen military surplus JN-4 Jenny aircraft, and operated out of an airfield in what would eventually be known as Fridley. It employed a team of local pilots, including Charles "Speed" Holman, who would go on to establish himself as something of a legend in Minnesota aviation circles. Hinck bought out Dodge and another partner less than a year after the company was incorporated. Before long, the Federated Fliers were becoming best known for their aerial thrill shows. Hinck was the mastermind of the operation.

Aerial stunts may have been the prime attraction of Hinck's shows, but they shared billing with several more earthbound exhibitions. The shows often opened with a motorcycle race or a running of whippets. Then they would move on to even bigger crowd-pleasers like automobile push-ball, an event in which two stripped-down Model Ts battled each other to bump an eight-foot inflated ball over a goal line. Only when all the terrestrial feats were complete would the air show begin. At first, the aerial portion followed a fairly standard script, with the obligatory stunt flying, wing walking, and parachute jumping, but as time

"Minnesota owes much of its aviation heritage to an elite group of pioneers who put aviation on the front page... Clarence Hinck was one of those pioneers who just had the entrepreneurial spirit and the gregarious nature that could make almost anything happen."

—Noel Allard, Minnesota aviation historian

went on, Hinck and his daredevils got more creative. In the 1930s, they added a new grandstand event known as the "house crash," in which pilots flew their planes into makeshift structures and deliberately sheared off their wings on strategically placed telephone poles.

Aerial thrill shows eventually fell out of favor, and the Federated Fliers stopped flying. Hinck turned his attention to other aerial pursuits. As a new war raged in Europe, Hinck landed a federal government contract to train pilots at Wold-Chamberlain Field (later known as Minneapolis–St. Paul International Airport). In 1941, he secured another contract to train glider pilots north of the Twin Cities, in Monticello. After the war, he switched to running a flying school for civilians—first at Wold-Chamberlain, then in Monticello, and finally at the airport in suburban Crystal.

When Hinck died in 1966 at the age of seventy-six, his obituary said nothing about his connection to Dunwoody, but perhaps it should have. If he hadn't trained in aviation mechanics at Dunwoody's naval school, he might never have gained the skills he needed to become a success in the flying business. Seventy-two years after he attended, his Dunwoody experience received prominent mention in the biography that accompanied his induction into the Minnesota Aviation Hall of Fame.

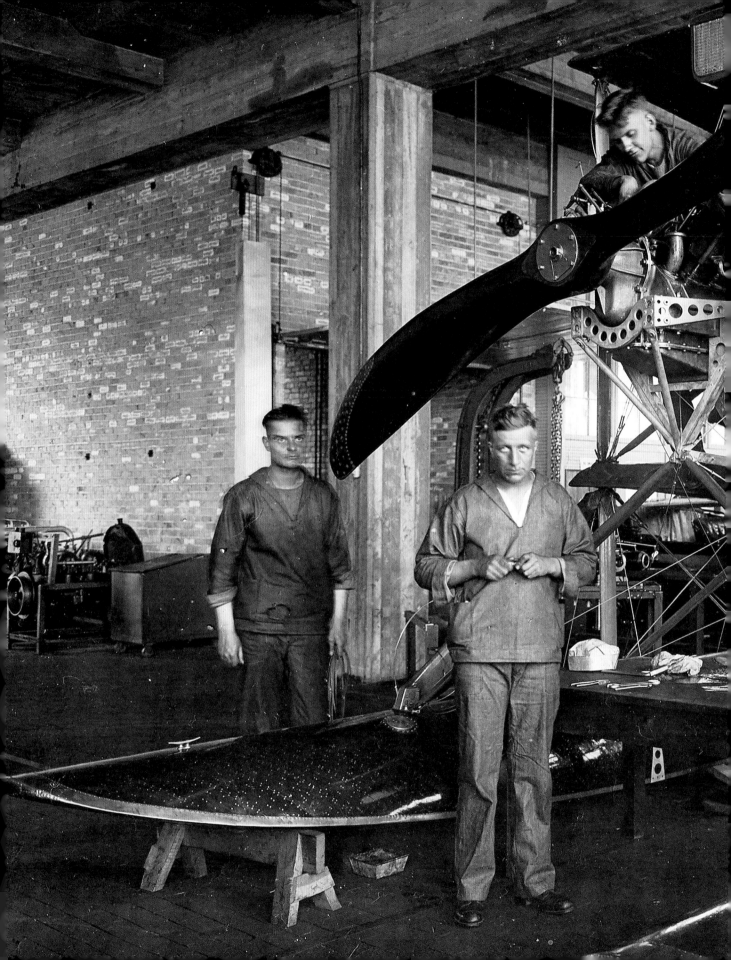

Aviation cadets at Dunwoody's "Naval School," 1918

Aviatio
droplan

180

GARY JANISCH

Architectural Drafting & Estimating, 1968

In 1983, Gary Janisch was in his mid-thirties, and was already thinking about retirement. In the fourteen years since graduating from Dunwoody's Architectural Drafting & Estimating program, he had spent nearly his entire career with a single company, Fabcon, a Savage, Minnesota–based manufacturer of precast concrete walls used in commercial and industrial buildings. He had risen quickly through the ranks, and had played a critical sales and marketing role in turning Fabcon into one of the largest precast concrete companies in the United States. During the course of his work there, he had spotted a business opportunity. "I was working with customers building apartments, condominiums, warehouses, big commercial buildings, but no one was building the little strip shopping centers," he recalled. "So, I asked the Fabcon board if it would be okay if I invested in or built some of these shopping centers for my retirement someday. They said, 'Sure!'"

With the board's blessing, Janisch teamed up with Jerry Hertel, an investment banker with Juran and Moody, who had funded multiple deals for Fabcon clients. They called their new company HJ Development. For their first project, Janisch and Hertel identified a site at a busy intersection in Savage. Then came the moment of truth. "I didn't have the money," Janisch said. "So, I took a second mortgage on my house. My wife asked me if I knew what I was doing, and I said, 'Sure!' But I was nervous." With financing in hand, Janisch and Hertel set to work building their first shopping center. The strip was to be anchored by a familiar tenant—a Tom Thumb convenience store.

Their choice of anchor tenant made sense. Convenience stores had been growing in popularity since the 1960s, due in large part to their low overhead, simplified shopping experience, extended hours of operation, and convenient locations, usually on busy traffic corners. In the Twin Cities, Tom Thumbs were by far the most numerous. With Tom Thumb as an anchor tenant, Janisch and Hertel were confident their investment would pay off.

An HJ Development property in Roseville.

They were right.

"We started with the first one, and we did well, and then we did the next one," Janisch recalled. "All of a sudden, a number of banks wanted to finance our projects, realizing we knew what we were doing." In the years that followed, Janisch and Hartel developed five more Tom Thumb–anchored shopping centers in Burnsville, Shakopee, Eden Prairie, Coon Rapids, and Anoka. Tom Thumb eventually faltered as big-box retailers moved into the Twin Cities market and larger grocery stores started staying open later, but by then, HJ Development had begun to diversify and strengthen its tenant mix.

In 1998, after twenty-seven years with Fabcon, Janisch decided to retire just before age fifty, and manage his and HJ Development's portfolio. He sold his Fabcon shares back to the company and spent his free time over the next eighteen months fishing and golfing and traveling with his wife. But he was still only in his early fifties, and he concluded that retirement didn't really suit him. "I thought, this is not the way it's supposed to be," he said. "So, I decided to build up the portfolio." HJ Development expanded its focus to include a broader mix of retail and office properties. By 2023, the company's fortieth-anniversary year, its portfolio boasted more than forty shopping centers and close to four hundred tenants, including national chains like Walmart, Cub Foods, Best Buy, Hobby Lobby, Panera Bread, Caribou Coffee, Starbucks, and medical clinics.

Janisch hadn't planned on becoming a commercial real estate developer while attending Dunwoody in the late 1960s, but as the years passed, he came to believe that his Dunwoody experience was a crucial factor in his success in that field. "I left there prepared for the outside," he said. "I learned structural design and much more. I learned to be on time, to get projects done. Dunwoody taught me a lot more than I ever expected. It taught me a little bit of everything. Without Dunwoody, I wouldn't be where I am today."

"Dunwoody taught me a lot more than I ever expected. It taught me a little bit of everything. Without Dunwoody, I wouldn't be where I am today."

—Gary Janisch

Lee Jessen (right) works with a high school newspaper editor.

LEE JESSEN

Printing & Graphics Technology, 1953

During the 1960s and 1970s, the student newspaper at St. Louis Park High School, the *Echo*, counted among its staff an impressive array of kids who would go on to become accomplished journalists—among them: *New York Times* reporter and columnist Thomas Friedman; film critic Marshall Fine; WCCO-TV sportscaster Mark Rosen; and FOX 9 newscaster Jeff Passolt. The *Echo* was printed twice a month at a small St. Louis Park shop called Curle Printing. And over the years, many of the students who cycled on and off its staff—including some of those who ended up going to work in big-city newsrooms—made excursions to Curle Printing to learn the art of newspaper layout. Their instructor during those field trips was the company's owner, a graduate of Dunwoody's Printing & Graphics program named Lee Jessen. And they were in good company. Jessen handled the printing not only of the *Echo*, but also of newspapers at a number of other local high schools, including Robbinsdale, Edina, and Minneapolis Washburn and South.

"It was really fun for him," his son Mark recalled. "It was his classroom."

Jessen knew firsthand how a young person could catch the printing bug. He had taken a junior high printing course while growing up in South Minneapolis, and almost from the moment he started that class, he was sure he wanted to become a printer. When he asked the instructor how best to pursue his dream, the instructor recommended he aim for Dunwoody's Printing program. Jessen picked up an ice delivery route and started saving money for tuition. By the summer after he graduated high school, he had the money he needed. He enrolled at Dunwoody and started classes in the fall of 1948.

As it turned out, it took Jessen longer than he had hoped to get started in his new career. Six months before he was scheduled to graduate, he was drafted into the U.S. Army. After his discharge two years later, he returned to Dunwoody and finished his training with financial help from the GI Bill.

During the first ten years of his career, Jessen worked for other people—first at a venerable Minneapolis printing company called Mono-trade, and then at Curle Printing, a younger and smaller shop in the City's Linden Hills neighborhood. At Curle, Jessen became a jack-of-all-trades, handling everything from typesetting to customer relations. When the company fell on hard times in 1963, he bought it from the owner, determined to save it. "He negotiated with all of the vendors to give him enough runway to turn things around," son Mark recalled. "He was able to do that. Everyone kept their jobs. He grew the business from there."

After spending about five years in the same location, Jessen moved the company into a new space in St. Louis Park and anchored it with a new, thirty-six-inch, one-color press. Then he traded in that press for a state-of-the-art two-color machine. When linotype gave way to computer typesetting, he became an early adopter of the new technology. His client list expanded, and included all those high school newspapers whose young staff members came to him for training in page layout. At its height, Curle employed about ten people— "just the way he liked it," Mark said. In 1995, Mark bought the company from his father and renamed it Jessen Press.

In his retirement, Jessen reconnected with Dunwoody and, as president of the College's Alumni Board of Managers, worked to reconnect others as well. His pride in Dunwoody remained constant in the years that followed. "[It] had opportunities for people who didn't mind getting their hands dirty," he said. "Dunwoody gave me the confidence and the skills I needed to succeed in business."

"Dunwoody gave me the confidence and the skills I needed to succeed in business."

—Lee Jessen

Lee Jessen (bottom) gained printing experience while serving in the U.S. Army and, after reenrolling at Dunwoody following his discharge, often shared his knowledge with his classmates.

JAY JOHNSON

NEI, Electronic Systems Technology, 1978

As the teenage son of the owner of two Amoco gas stations in Northeast Minneapolis, Jay Johnson was expected to pitch in at one or the other location whenever he wasn't in school or participating in athletics. That meant he spent a lot of time studying for classes there—first during high school, and then while he attended Northwestern Electronics Institute (NEI), a technical college that later merged with Dunwoody. One Friday evening during the summer of 1978, Johnson was working at his father's station at Broadway and Adams when he checked under the hood of a car a customer had brought in for a fill-up. He noticed a leak, and informed the customer that his water pump was on the verge of failing. The customer, who was heading out of town for the weekend, asked Johnson if he could do anything about it. Johnson told him he could. It just so happened he had a replacement pump inside, he said. He could have the customer on the road in no time. About an hour later, during checkout, the grateful customer noticed an NEI textbook that Johnson had set aside.

"Who's studying electronics?" he asked.

Johnson replied that he was.

"Interesting," the customer said. "How would you like to have a job interview?"

As it turned out, the customer was a district manager for Burroughs Computer Systems, an early technology firm that later merged with Sperry UNIVAC to create Unisys. A few days after swapping out the customer's water pump, Johnson went in for an interview. Within the week, he was employed at Burroughs as a field engineer, fixing broken equipment for the company's banking clients. His days of manning his father's Amoco stations were over.

In 2003, Dunwoody merged with NEI College of Technology.

Johnson had long been fascinated with how things worked and how they didn't (by his reckoning, he had, as a young boy, taken apart at least four alarm clocks to find out what made them tick—without always figuring out how to put them back together), and his proclivity for identifying problems and solving them served him well as he rose through the ranks at Burroughs and Unisys. Along the way, his work with banking clients led him to develop valuable expertise in IT security. Among his first big security challenges was a problem that's still with us today: forgotten passwords. When Johnson first started working with bank clients, retrieving passwords required physical trips to a mainframe computer. Then Johnson figured out that he could skip the trips and just "sniff the password" by tapping into the wires leading from mainframe to terminal. But with that insight came the realization that networks might be more vulnerable than he ever thought. "Little did I know," he said, "that that would lead me into the world of security."

In 1995, Johnson left Unisys to develop banking security packages for GE Capital. About a year later, he left GE and partnered with a former Unisys colleague, Jay Chaudhry, to start SecureIT, a provider of internet security applications. Their timing was impeccable. In 1998, he and Chaudhry sold SecureIT to the digital certificate software company VeriSign for $50 million.

Just twenty years before that, Johnson had landed his first job in the technology sector, thanks in large part to a satisfied gas station customer who noticed he was studying electronics at NEI. But that unlikely connection was not the only reason Johnson valued his NEI education. "It gave me a great understanding of how technology works," he said. "It gave me the ability to explore what makes it tick."

Johnson's appreciation for the training he received at NEI led him to forge an increasingly close relationship to Dunwoody, the college with which it eventually merged. Among other things, he established several scholarships to encourage students from his alma mater, Edison High School, to attend Dunwoody. "I decided my cohorts at Edison should understand that there are more choices than just the U of M and St. Thomas and Augsburg," he said. "Great things can come out of Dunwoody as well."

"I decided my cohorts at Edison should understand that there are more choices than just the U of M and St. Thomas and Augsburg. Great things can come out of Dunwoody as well."

—Jay Johnson

CECIL JONES

Electrical, 1922

Cecil Jones grew up on a farm in Blue Earth County, Minnesota, but he knew from an early age that he didn't want to be a farmer. In 1920, he left high school early to enroll at Dunwoody Institute under a program that allowed him to finish his secondary education while simultaneously learning a trade. Two years later, he completed Dunwoody's Electrical curriculum (it took him a little longer to earn his high school diploma), and headed back to Blue Earth County to start his off-the-farm career. His first job was apparently with an electrical repair shop in Mankato. But at some point during the early to mid-1920s, he moved to nearby Lake Crystal and opened a shop of his own. It was there that he thought up the invention that became the foundation of his later success.

Jones had left the farm, but the farm hadn't completely left him. Although he had traded in his overalls for a suit and tie, he was still familiar with the joys and hardships of rural life, and many, if not most, of his customers were farmers. He knew, for example, that rural areas had fallen far behind the big cities in terms of access to reliable electricity, and he also knew that power gap made it hard for farmers to take full advantage of one of modern life's technological advances: the radio.

In those days before widespread rural electrification, many farms relied on low-power direct current (DC) supplied by an in-house "lighting plant"—essentially a kerosene-powered generator connected to a bank of bulky storage batteries. The radios made for those DC systems were inferior to "city radios" that ran on more powerful alternating current (AC), and many farmers longed for the day when they could listen to the same type of clear-signal broadcasts that city folk already enjoyed.

Early ad for Cecil Jones's "Kato Konverter."

Jones shared his customers' frustration with the radio divide, and he set out to bridge it. The invention he came up with was a rotary converter that made it possible for farmers to plug superior AC radios into their existing DC systems. In 1929, he and two partners founded a new company, Kato Engineering in Mankato, and started manufacturing "Kato Konverters" for rural markets. Five years later, he bought out his partners and took over as president, a position he would hold for more than forty years.

Kato Engineering grew into a major Mankato employer during World War II, when it landed a contract to make electric generators for the U.S. Army. The company continued to grow after the war by shifting its focus to the commercial and residential markets. By the mid-1950s, Kato's product line included generators of many types, rotary converters, motors, and telephone ringing power machines. Its sales regions stretched across the United States and into many overseas markets as well.

By that time, Kato had spun off two subsidiaries: Jones Sheet Metal (later renamed Jones Metal Products), founded initially to fabricate housings for Kato's generators; and Katolight, a maker of standby power units. The three companies combined employed thousands of Mankato workers over the years, and remained family-owned enterprises until Jones' death in 1976. In the years that followed, the family sold two of them—Kato Engineering and Katolight. The third, Jones Metal Products, continued on as a closely held company run by three successive female leaders: Jones's wife, Mildred; their daughter, Marsha Richards; and their granddaughter, Sarah Richards.

Jones had left the farm in 1920, knowing only that he didn't want to spend the rest of his life tending crops and livestock. His training at Dunwoody had given him the skills he needed to return to Blue Earth County and become one of Mankato's most successful entrepreneurs. "Somehow he learned that Dunwoody would provide the education he needed to learn a trade and complete his high school," daughter Marsha Richards said. "He was very proud of his Dunwoody experience."

"**Somehow he learned that Dunwoody would provide the education he needed to learn a trade and complete his high school. He was very proud of his Dunwoody experience.**"

—Marsha Richards on her father, Cecil Jones

Ken Konrad on the repair ship USS *Tutuila*, around 1967.

KEN KONRAD

Machine Tool Technology, 1964

On October 12, 2000, a small boat pulled alongside the U.S. Navy destroyer USS *Cole*, which had stopped for fueling in the port of Aden, Yemen. The boat's pilots waved at several sailors aboard the ship. No one seemed too concerned that anything was amiss. But then the boat exploded. The blast ripped a forty-foot-wide hole in the *Cole*, killing seventeen crew members and injuring thirty-nine. Terrorists had exposed a serious flaw in U.S. naval defenses. The U.S. Navy responded by increasing protection of its ships in port. That meant, among other things, upgrading the fleet of small patrol boats it relied on to provide close-to-shore defense for its larger warships. But there was a problem: most of those patrol boats were equipped with stern drives that were not made to withstand the near-constant use that would now be required. The Navy needed a new supplier.

It turned to a small company in Hudson, Wisconsin, called Konrad Marine.

Ken Konrad had started his namesake company in 1991, after nearly a quarter century in the machining business, and it had been something of a circuitous journey. After graduating from high school, he attended St. Thomas College and promptly flunked out. Then he enrolled in Dunwoody's Machine Tool program and graduated in 1964 near the top of his class. Not long after that, he joined the U.S. Navy as a machinist, and, during his second year of active duty, served on a tender servicing patrol boats in Vietnam. After his discharge, he returned to the Twin Cities, and opened his own small machine shop. Unsatisfied with the subcontract work he was doing, he mothballed his equipment, enrolled at the University of Minnesota, and graduated three and a half years later, in 1973, with a degree in mechanical engineering. From there, he landed at the Minneapolis manufacturer Graco, where he worked as an engineer for three years. But he still yearned to be his own boss. In 1976, he quit Graco and started his own company, Konrad Corporation.

In the years that followed, Konrad grew his St. Paul–based company into a successful maker of parts for steel mills. In 1987, the firm, which by then employed sixteen people, moved to a much larger facility in Hudson. But the cyclical ups and downs of the steel industry were hard to take, and Konrad set out to diversify. At the suggestion of one of his sales representatives, he turned to a field with which he already had some experience, thanks to his time in the Navy: marine propulsion. In 1991, he started Konrad Marine as a supplier of stern drive components and assemblies. A year later, the new company introduced its first complete manufactured stern drive. As the years went on, Konrad Marine earned a reputation as one of the world's premier manufacturers of dependable, durable, and long-lasting stern drives capable of handling the torque of diesel engines.

That reputation made Konrad Marine the logical choice when the U.S. Navy rushed to upgrade its patrol boat fleet in the wake of the USS *Cole* attack. Orders for the company's Konrad 520 stern drive started arriving in waves. In 2002, sales and profits soared as the Navy bought up almost everything Konrad produced. The burst of business helped put the company on solid financial footing, and made it possible to keep manufacturing ever more sophisticated stern drives for commercial and military watercraft, while expanding into markets around the globe.

Looking back on the circuitous route his career had taken, Ken Konrad could see that most of the stops he had made were crucial, but he believed none was more important than the one he made at Dunwoody. "When I started full-time in the business, I was a Dunwoody graduate and I was a graduate of the University of Minnesota with an engineering degree," he said. "But during those first couple of years, that business depended most on my experience at Dunwoody. I don't think I would have made it if I had just been a mechanical engineer. In fact, I know I wouldn't have."

"During those first couple of years, [my] business depended most on my experience at Dunwoody. I don't think I would have made it if I had just been a mechanical engineer. In fact, I know I wouldn't have."

—Ken Konrad

Figure B: 600B Series X-Dimension Guidlines

Schematic of one of Konrad Marine's many stern drives.

HAROLD LATHROP

Highway Department, early 1920s

Lathrop State Park is about an hour's drive south of Pueblo, Colorado, nestled in the shadow of a pair of mountains known as the Spanish Peaks. Established in 1962, Lathrop is Colorado's first state park, more than 1,500 acres encompassing a pair of recreational lakes, a golf course, and two campgrounds—one with full amenities and one rustic. It also seems to be the only state park in the United States named after a Dunwoody graduate.

Harold Lathrop was born in Wisconsin but grew up in Minneapolis. After serving in the U.S. Navy during World War I, he returned home to Minnesota and went to work for his father's candy company, a predecessor of what would become Kemps Ice Cream. But Lathrop apparently did not envision a future in the candy business. Instead, he pursued higher education—first at Dunwoody, in what was then known as the institute's Highway Department, and then at the University of Minnesota's School of Engineering.

Lathrop's training at Dunwoody and the U of M apparently served him well. He landed a job with the Minneapolis Park Board in 1924, and eventually became an apprentice to Theodore Wirth, the City's visionary superintendent of parks. During his time with the park board, Lathrop worked closely with Wirth on the planning of many public spaces, including Wold-Chamberlain Field (now Minneapolis–St. Paul International Airport). In 1929, he returned to Dunwoody to deliver a speech about the airport's progress to a group of appreciative alumni. Lathrop stayed with the park board until 1934, when he left to oversee a slew of state park projects funded by President Franklin D. Roosevelt's New Deal. The following year, he was named the first director of Minnesota's state park system, then known as the State Parks Division of the Minnesota Department of Conservation.

The entrance to Colorado's Lathrop State Park.

Lathrop became a passionate advocate for Minnesota's parks. In a series of articles in *Minnesota Conservation Volunteer* magazine, he urged his fellow Minnesotans to experience and enjoy the State's public spaces, while making sure to share them responsibly with others. "Such consideration will give posterity the same opportunity for enjoyment in these natural environments as are yours," he wrote. He believed Minnesota possessed "the finest of natural attributes," and would soon earn a place "in the foreground as a vacation land." He had a standard definition for an "ideal" state park:

> A typical portion of the state's original domain of adequate size, of which a small portion may be set aside for concentrated use, and the remainder preserved in a primeval condition, accessible only by a system of foot trails and waterways, in which present and future generations may study the flora, fauna, and geologic structures of nature, unspoilt, unimproved, and unbeautified.

It was a definition that would stand up well for many years to come.

Lathrop remained with Minnesota's State Park system throughout the final years of the Great Depression and through all of World War II. In 1946, after twelve years at the division's helm, he headed west to begin the next stage of his career. Over the following decade, he worked as a western states field consultant for the National Recreation Association, an organization that advocated for a broad range of recreational activities, including physical fitness, sports, and performing arts. But eventually, he returned to the field in which he had built his career: state parks management. In 1957, he was named the first director of Colorado's Parks and Recreation Department. It was a position he held until 1961, when he died of a heart attack at the age of sixty.

When his namesake park south of Pueblo was dedicated the year after his death, Lathrop was lauded as the "father" of Colorado's state park system. Apparently, no one suggested at that time that he deserved similar accolades for his work in Minnesota. But perhaps it was just an oversight resulting from the passage of time. Today he's all but forgotten in the state where he first made his name—except maybe at Dunwoody, the school that set him on course for his long parks career.

"**Minnesota has the finest of natural attributes as a tourist state, and we are just beginning to harvest the fruits of the efforts made for the last few years to put Minnesota in the foreground as a vacation land.**"

—Harold Lathrop in *Minnesota Conservationist*, June 1936

AUSTIN LUTZ

Automotive Service Technology, 2002

Austin Lutz was not your classic gearhead. "I didn't know I wanted to work on cars at all," he would later say, looking back on his teenage years. "I didn't grow up tearing cars apart or anything like that." Even when he landed his first job at the age of fifteen at an Amoco gas station in Hopkins, he worked in the front of the store as a cashier rather than in the garage, where grease tended to get under fingernails. Then, one day a manager asked if he wanted to become an oil changer. Lutz asked if the job paid better than what he was earning at the cash register. The manager told him it paid a dollar an hour more. "I said, 'All right!'" Lutz recalled. "'Sign me up!'"

Thus started Austin Lutz's career in the field of what he called "turning wrenches."

Lutz's garage work at the Amoco station allowed him to gain valuable car repair skills, but he knew he would need more training if he was going to make progress on what looked to be a viable career path. While still a student at Hopkins High School, he took several automotive courses at Hennepin Technical College. Then, after a brief postsecondary enrollment at Penn State University ("I did not like it at all"), he returned home and asked the owner of another Hopkins auto shop for career advice. "What he told me," Lutz later recalled, "was if I was serious about automotive, I had to go to Dunwoody."

Lutz enrolled in Dunwoody's Automotive Service Technology program in 2000, attending classes during the day while working night shifts at a Goodyear station in Champlin. But when he graduated two years later, he still wasn't completely sure he wanted to spend the rest of his life turning wrenches. "I'm not saying I didn't enjoy it," he later said of the work. "I just knew I didn't want to be in the back of the shop, full-time, forever." He continued on as a student, taking general education courses at Normandale Community College, and earning a four-year degree in agricultural and food business management at the University of Minnesota. But after working for less than a year in the agricultural sector, he realized it wasn't the right fit for him.

In 2007, Lutz started teaching classes as an adjunct automotive instructor at Dunwoody. For nearly a decade, he helped students much like he had been train to make careers for themselves as automotive technicians. But eventually, he started thinking about opening his own shop. "I had a full toolbox at my house, and I was fixing cars on the side," he said. "I enjoyed it. So, I decided to start looking for an auto shop to buy or a space to lease." In 2015, he took over the lease of a longtime mechanic in Minnetonka, not far from his old Hopkins stomping grounds. He called his new shop BAM! Automotive.

Unlike many first-time auto shop owners, Lutz decided not to specialize. BAM! would service almost any make and model, just as long as it wasn't too new or too old. "I felt there wasn't really a good general automotive company out there," he explained. "So, I thought fixing everything would be my niche." His first few years in business featured "a whole lot of learning and a whole lot of doing it wrong," but, with the help of a business coach, he eventually found his footing. By 2022, BAM! was doing so well that he felt confident enough to open a second location in St. Louis Park.

It had taken Lutz about fifteen years from the day he first started turning wrenches to the day he opened BAM!, but by the time he finally did, he felt he was ready. And he gave Dunwoody a lot of credit for that. "Someone needs to drive home the basic concepts of how to think through problems," he said. "And that's something that Dunwoody does fantastically well."

BAM! Automotive opened a second location in St. Louis Park, Minnesota.

"Someone needs to drive home the basic concepts of how to think through problems, and that's something that Dunwoody does fantastically well."

—Austin Lutz

BENITO MATIAS

Engineering Drafting & Design, 1993

On one of the first days of classes during the summer of 2023 at Ascension Catholic School in North Minneapolis, Principal Benito Matias was called outside to address a delicate matter. A young boy, a rising first grader, was on the playground, screaming inconsolably, refusing to join his classmates inside. "He was not having a good morning," Matias later recalled with considerable understatement. The boy's mother was there, but she had to leave for work. Matias, sensing her growing anxiety, assured her that he would personally look after her son until the situation resolved. Once she was gone, Matias carried the boy, still kicking and screaming, inside. "I knew it couldn't last forever," he said. He held the youngster and soothed him with calming words for about ten minutes as the sobs and screams subsided. After some coaxing, the boy revealed the source of his distress: he had left his favorite toy, a Robin (Batman's Boy Wonder) action figure, at home. Matias possessed no replacement Robins, but he did have another similar toy that he hoped would keep the peace. He gave it to the child. The remaining tension immediately dissipated. A few minutes later, the young scholar (the preferred term at Ascension) headed off to class, his troubles left behind. Matias could only shake his head in amusement, having successfully managed yet another mini crisis. "Forty minutes earlier," he said, "folks would have thought somebody was trying to kill that boy, given the way he was screaming and yelling."

Unlike many educators, Matias had never received any formal training in how to help a distraught child cope with the absence of a beloved action figure, but that didn't mean he lacked the requisite skills to become a school administrator. As his morning spent consoling the scholar with the missing Robin demonstrated, he had plenty. And, by his reckoning, he had gained at least some of his most relevant skills at an unlikely place: his alma mater, Dunwoody College.

"It's odd to think that going to Dunwoody for engineering design would in any shape or form prepare me for this morning," he said. "But it's not about the training. It's about the people."

Matias had never heard of Dunwoody before 1988, when, as a high school freshman, he joined the first cohort of students in what was then known as the Youth Career Awareness Program (YCAP). Dunwoody had started YCAP with the goal of introducing under-represented students—especially students of color—to the academic requirements of technical school. The program exposed Matias to career possibilities he had never dreamed of. It also introduced him to a man who became one of the greatest influences in his life: a part-time, African American counselor named Leon Rankin. Rankin was one of the driving forces behind YCAP, and he took Matias under his wing. After Matias graduated from high school and entered Dunwoody on a YCAP scholarship, his relationship with Rankin only grew closer. And that relationship continued after Matias completed Dunwoody's Engineering Drafting & Design program, and went on to work for the College in several roles, including as YCAP program manager and as executive director of Dunwoody Academy, a charter school the College sponsored from 2006 to 2011.

By then, Matias was well on his way to establishing what was to become a long career in education. His experience at Dunwoody Academy opened the door to new opportunities at Ascension Catholic School, first in an administrative support role, and eventually as principal. Through it all, he remained thankful for the lessons he learned at Dunwoody, and for the people there who helped shape his life—especially Leon Rankin. "Mr. Rankin never had to hold me while I was unconsolably crying," he said, "but he was someone who was consistent in my life in addition to my parents, someone who I looked up to, who I knew cared for me. All of those things have impact."

Benito Matias with a gym full of Ascension scholars.

"[Dunwoody instructor Leon Rankin] was someone who was consistent in my life in addition to my parents, someone who I looked up to, who I knew cared for me. All of those things have impact."

—Benito Matias

World War I Army training

Burt McGlynn serves Travl Bake customers, 1954.

BURT MCGLYNN

Baking, 1965

One morning in the spring of 1954, a large black and silver bus rumbled to a stop in a residential neighborhood of suburban St. Louis Park, Minnesota, wafting wonderful aromas and announcing its presence with shivering sleigh bells. The smells and sounds combined to have a pied piper effect. Curious residents emerged from their homes to investigate. As the crowd assembled, the driver of the bus, thirty-year-old Burt McGlynn, appeared at its door, holding out a tray of fresh-from-the-oven baked goods. He invited the curious inside, one by one, to see what was going on. What they found was a miniature bakery on wheels, complete with revolving oven, donut fryer, refrigerator, self-serve display case, and a harried baker working feverishly to turn out as many fresh-baked donuts, pies, cakes, and rolls as he could before the selling began. McGlynn informed his intrigued guests that his bus, the "Travl Bake," was a new business venture of McGlynn Bakeries, a Minneapolis company founded more than three decades earlier by his father, James (J. T.) McGlynn. The Travl Bake would be making regular stops in St. Louis Park, he said, delivering to homes what J. T. called "the one priceless ingredient in bakery products—freshness." Within minutes, all manner of baked goods started emptying from the bus's display case.

It didn't take long for the Travl Bake to generate all sorts of publicity for McGlynn, including a feature in the *Wall Street Journal.* Advertisements proclaimed that the traveling bakery was going to "make life better for everybody." But Burt McGlynn soon soured on the enterprise. "In some ways, it was kind of scary," he said. "A lot of kids would see the bus and come running out into the streets. I was afraid I might hit one of them." After about a year on the thoroughfares of St. Louis Park, the Travl Bake was retired. J. T. McGlynn started thinking about closing down his bakeries. But his son had other ideas. Burt had grown up in the bakery business, served as a naval baker during World War II, and given up a chance to go to college to help his father stay in business. He wasn't going to let the company die. In 1956, he bought out his father and started making plans to shift McGlynn Bakeries' focus. He had seen firsthand how well fresh baked goods were received in St. Louis Park. He intended to keep looking beyond Minneapolis's city limits.

"I figured I could get fresh bakery products into the bigger stores in the suburbs," he said.

In the years that followed, Burt McGlynn turned McGlynn Bakeries into one of the best-known brands in the Twin Cities. After selling the company to a competitor in 1958 and buying it back four years later, he finally followed through on his plan to bring fresh baked goods to the suburbs. He started by relaunching his business inside two of the first Target stores, in St. Louis Park and Crystal. By 1972, about three dozen Targets had their own McGlynn Bakeries inside. McGlynn Bakeries continued to grow through affiliations with other supermarket chains like SuperValu and Applebaum's. Over the years, Burt McGlynn also established several successful subsidiaries, including a pair of frozen baked goods companies (one of which was eventually sold to Pillsbury for about $135 million) and DecoPac, which grew into the world's largest marketer of professional cake decorations. The last of McGlynn's retail bakeries closed in 2001.

Sometimes lost in the stories of Burt McGlynn's personal and professional successes was the fact that, when he wanted to gain greater expertise in his field, he had turned to one of the best baking programs in the Country—one that happened to be located just a few miles from his old Travl Bake route in St. Louis Park. In the early 1960s, while McGlynn's affiliation with Target was still in its infancy, he had enrolled at Dunwoody Institute, hoping to strengthen his baking knowledge and, presumably, prepare himself for his company's upcoming expansion. Unlike most of his fellow classmates at the time, he was middle-aged and mid-career, a classic example of a continuing education student. But his later-in-life training apparently paid off. In the years immediately following his graduation from Dunwoody his company began its impressive ascent. More than three decades later, in 1999, the school at which he refined his skills recognized his accomplishments with its Alumni Entrepreneur Award.

It was in the years immediately following his graduation from Dunwoody that his company began its impressive ascent.

Cory and Collin Miller

CORY AND COLLIN MILLER

Machine Tool Technology, 1995 and 1995

It isn't uncommon for two people who agree with each other to describe themselves as being of the "same mind," but the term seems especially apt when applied to Dunwoody alumni Cory and Collin Miller. The Miller brothers are identical twins whose educational and career paths, running virtually in parallel, have led them into side-by-side executive positions with the company they have ownership in: AVID International Molding Solutions in Elk River, Minnesota. They may not be inseparable, but they're about as close as two brothers can get.

"I can honestly say he's my best friend," Collin said.

Cory concurs: "It's kind of nice to come to work with your best buddy."

It's been a lifelong journey in tandem for the Miller twins. After graduating from Burnsville High School in 1991, they enrolled together at the University of Minnesota to study mechanical engineering. But after two years of calculus, chemistry, and class sizes in the hundreds, they decided to switch course. "We needed something more hands-on," Cory explains. "Something that, at the end of the day, let us see we had produced a tangible result." Instead of continuing their studies at the U, they enrolled in Dunwoody's Machine Tool Technology program. Almost immediately, they knew they had made the right choice. "We were building on our skills as we learned," Cory said. "Everything made a lot more sense because we were seeing it in real-world applications."

The Millers could have headed off in different directions after graduating from Dunwoody in 1995, but that wasn't their way. ("We've always been kind of a package deal," Collin said.) They both accepted full-time positions with a New Hope die-casting firm called Tool Products, and began their new hands-on careers making molds. Over time, they honed their skills and moved into the management ranks. After nearly twelve years at Tool Products,

AVID International Molding Solutions' Elk River facility.

Cory jumped at an opportunity to work for what was then called E&O Tool and Plastics as a toolroom manager. A few months later, Collin followed him. As time went on, they joined the company's senior leadership team, and helped what is now known as AVID International Molding Solutions take a more aggressive stance in the marketplace. In 2015, they partnered with the son of the company's founder to become co-owners. Cory took over as president and CEO in 2018. Collin became director of engineering and tooling. Under this new leadership, AVID grew into a $35 million company—with more than 250 employees in Elk River and Monterrey, Mexico—specializing in thick wall molding for pressure vessel filtration. Its customers included 3M, Donaldson Corporation, John Deere, and Premium Sound Solutions.

These days, when the Millers look out on their facilities in Elk River and Monterrey, they see a direct connection to the hands-on training they received after leaving the U of M for Dunwoody. Their tooling background remains, in Collin's words, "the backbone of our entire engineering system."

Cory reinforces the point with a hypothetical.

"Let's say I wanted to get a management job at 3M," he said. "I couldn't. I don't check the boxes. I don't officially have a four-year degree. And yet I'm still in charge of a $35 million company with a great growth trajectory." As Cory sees it, the education he and his brother received at Dunwoody was invaluable, and has been a major factor in their success. "Regardless of whether you're in the HVAC program or tooling or whatever else, you'll come out of Dunwoody equipped to be successful in your business," he said. "You can go get those other skills down the road if need be. You can always get your four-year degree. You can always get your MBA. Bottom line is, when you come out of Dunwoody, you're never going to miss a meal. You're going to have a roof over your head. And you're going to have a well-paying job with a lot of upside."

"Bottom line is, when you come out of Dunwoody, you're never going to miss a meal. You're going to have a roof over your head. And you're going to have a well-paying job with a lot of upside."

—Cory Miller

MORT MORTENSON SR.

Building Construction, 1925

Mort Mortenson Sr. was what he would later describe as "the ripe old age of forty-eight" when he started his own construction firm, M. A. Mortenson Company, on April Fool's Day 1954—more than a quarter century after earning his Building Construction Certificate from Dunwoody Institute. Few Dunwoody alumni would ever be able to say they started their first successful business so late in life. But Mortenson was not one to back down from a challenge. "I think he just had a desire to do something on his own," his son, Mort Jr., later said. When Mortenson Sr. started his company out of his family's home in suburban Richfield, he was, in effect, making a huge bet on himself.

It took a while, but the bet paid off handsomely.

Mortenson Sr. was the son of Swedish immigrants, and spent much of his boyhood growing up in Minneapolis, where his father, Nels, was a construction superintendent with James Leck Company. In his teens, the younger Mortenson worked at various jobs on his father's projects, and took a liking to the construction business. After first enrolling as a structural engineering student at the University of Minnesota, he switched to Dunwoody, and finished the Building Construction program in 1925. When an early attempt to start his own construction company failed (it was the height of the Great Depression), he landed a job at his father's employer, James Leck. In the two decades that followed, Mortenson Sr. was called on to supervise increasingly complex projects, most of them overseen by James Leck and its successor company, D'Arcy Leck Construction. By 1954, he figured he had racked up more than enough experience to go off on his own. "I knew that it would take some breaks along the way," he said. "But where there's risk, there's also a lot of opportunity."

M. A. Mortenson Company's first job was a remodeling project for Minneapolis's Paul Bunyan Bait Company.

The newly incorporated M. A. Mortenson Company landed its first job—a $370 remodeling project for Minneapolis's Paul Bunyan Bait Company—during its first few months in business. By year's end, it had eight projects valued at over $400,000 on the books. It moved out of the Mortensons' Richfield rambler and into its own office in downtown Minneapolis. From there, the company continued to grow, and the projects it took on got bigger and bigger. Over time, it developed a reputation for superior work on a variety of public and private construction projects, including hospitals, schools, and power plants. Much of its success was due to Mortenson's emphasis on repeat business—a determination to, in his words, "build so well that an owner will invite us back for additional work." By the late 1960s, the company was on the verge of cracking a widely respected list of the four hundred largest construction firms in the United States. Mortenson, then sixty-two, decided it was time to step down. In 1969, his thirty-two-year-old son, Mort Jr., succeeded him as president.

In retirement, Mortenson Sr. marveled at how the company he started in his Richfield home grew into an emerging local, regional, and national juggernaut under Mort Jr.'s leadership. When a family friend asked if he was proud of what his son was accomplishing, Mortenson Sr. just smiled and said, "I sure hope he knows what he's doing." When the elder Mortenson died in 1986, he had only an inkling of how big the company would become. By the time Mort Jr. handed the company's reins to *his* son, David, in 2015, M. A. Mortenson Company ranked as the sixteenth-largest general contractor in the United States.

Although Mortenson Sr. was the only member of his immediate family to attend Dunwoody, his connection with the school extended over generations. Under the leadership of both Mort Jr. and son David, M. A. Mortenson Company maintained strong links with Dunwoody, as did the Mortenson family themselves. The company supported the College financially and through the volunteer work of its employees. Many Dunwoody graduates went on to work there. And Alice Mortenson, wife of Mort Jr., served on the school's Board of Trustees from 1987 to 1997. The connection may have started with Mort Sr.'s attendance back in the 1920s, but it is still going strong a century later. "We have a very close, collaborative relationship," David Mortenson said. "We view Dunwoody as a really important educator in the fabric of the industry and in the fabric of the Twin Cities."

"I knew that it would take some breaks along the way, but where there's risk, there's also a lot of opportunity."

—Mort Mortenson Sr.

Jack Mowry

JACK MOWRY

Engineering Drafting & Design, 1971

In the year 2000, at the age of fifty-five, Jack Mowry bought a forty-foot sloop, *Breagan*, with the intention of sailing it around the world from its home port in Bayfield, Wisconsin. To those who didn't know him well, the purchase might have looked like a souped-up response to a classic midlife crisis, a sign that he was ready to move on from Metal Craft and Riverside Machining and Engineering, the pair of successful businesses he had started over the previous two decades. But that wasn't the case at all. Once he began sailing across oceans and seas—the Atlantic, the Mediterranean, the Caribbean, the Pacific—Mowry found he could never truly leave his businesses behind. "Up until the very end, he would call the shop and talk to the controller," recalled his daughter, Trish, who, with her brother, Sean, assumed ownership of the companies in 2005. "And then, when the weather got too bad or it was winter or hurricane season, he'd dry-dock the boat and fly home. And when he was back, he was always at work—not necessarily *doing* work, but *at* work—checking up on us."

Like many successful entrepreneurs, Jack Mowry lived his business.

A product of Pine City, Minnesota, and Howard, South Dakota, Mowry began his business journey during the late 1960s by enrolling in a six-month Tool & Die program at Dunwoody, and then returning to complete a two-year degree in Engineering Drafting & Design. After concluding that he actually preferred machining over drafting, he went to work for several years as a machinist at a couple of Twin Cities area shops. Then he struck out on his own. In 1973, he started Metal Craft in the basement of a strip mall in Elk River, Minnesota, with a manual mill and a manual lathe. Among his earliest contracts was to make and assemble parts for concrete drills. Without a dedicated workforce to do the finishing, he brought the parts home and paid his kids a small wage to assemble them while they watched TV.

"And then we'd get faster and faster at it, and we'd get more and more done, and he kept dropping the price," his daughter, Trish, recalled. "He'd say, 'You guys are too fast! I can't pay you that much!'"

Before too long, though, Metal Craft was doing well enough to move into its own five-thousand-square-foot building. Around 1990, Mowry, anticipating a growing demand among aging baby boomers for knee and hip replacements, began retooling his company to make close-tolerance parts for surgical instruments. Its client list expanded to include medical companies like Medtronic, American Medical Systems, and Zimmer Spine. Then, in 1996, Mowry acquired the engineering subsidiary of one of Metal Craft's existing clients, Cray Research of Chippewa Falls, Wisconsin, and turned it into Riverside Machining and Engineering, a specialist in brazing and precision machining, primarily serving defense industries. By then, Trish and Sean had joined the business and were being groomed to take over from their father—if he ever decided to retire.

By the time Mowry started sailing *Breagan* around the world and taking his first (reluctant) steps toward retirement, he had built what started out as a one-man machine shop into a pair of companies with about a hundred employees and more than $8 million in combined annual sales. In the years that followed, he watched with pride as Metal Craft and Riverside grew at an even more accelerated pace under the leadership of his son and daughter. He continued to fill his days with sailing and other outside interests, like collecting and restoring classic cars, but his companies never strayed far from his mind. And through it all, he continued to credit his alma mater for at least part of his success. "Dunwoody gave me confidence," he said. "When I left there, I had no doubt I could do whatever I wanted to do."

Jack Mowry started Metal Craft in the basement of a strip mall with a manual mill and lathe.

"Dunwoody gave me confidence. When I left there, I had no doubt I could do whatever I wanted to do."

—Jack Mowry

Ray and Nylene Newkirk at the presentation of the
2016 William and Kate Dunwoody Philanthropist Award.

RAY NEWKIRK

Machine Tool Technology, 1965

If you want to understand Ray Newkirk's success in the business world, consider Bugles.

In the mid-1960s, Minneapolis-based General Mills decided to jump into the snack food business with a potato chip alternative that it described as "a crunchy little horn that tastes like corn." Bugles, as the little snacks were known, were formed from sheets of dough made of yellow cornmeal and a few other simple ingredients. But those sheets had to be cut into little triangles before the Bugles could become Bugles. That's where Ray Newkirk came in.

Newkirk was a former student of Dunwoody's evening Machine Tool program, and in 1965, he started his own machine shop, Tape Inc., to do the kind of specialized tooling—cutting, shaping, and forming—that General Mills needed to turn out its new horn-shaped snacks. Tape Inc.'s contribution to the Bugle-making process was just one part of a long production line, but it was a crucial part. "You have to sheet the dough," Newkirk explained. "Then you must cut and shape it. It's just like making Christmas cookies at home, only you do it on a high-production basis." The rotary dies that Newkirk manufactured for General Mills helped establish Tape Inc. as an innovative tool-and-die shop, and highlighted one of Newkirk's strengths as a business owner: his ability to solve problems and seize opportunities when they presented themselves. "I'm an opportunist," he said. "I love to find ways to solve problems for customers."

Newkirk had recognized early on that the world of machining and tooling was in the process of becoming "numerically controlled" by binary code tape (in other words, computerized), and he aimed to take advantage of that new technology—hence the name Tape Inc. After about three years in business, the company had earned enough money to start investing in that technology and begin expanding. Its rotary die expertise helped it land lucrative contracts with other major companies, including Procter & Gamble, which needed

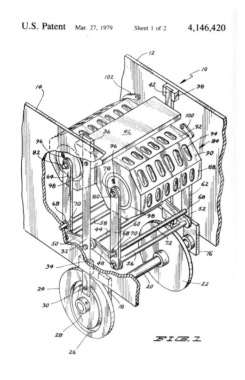

Ray Newkirk was awarded multiple patents over the course of his career, including one for a "Rotary Sealing Machine for Thermoplastic Articles."

dies for cutting, among other things, disposable diapers, and 3M, for cutting sandpaper discs. During the late 1960s, Newkirk improved a process for fusion bonding thermoplastics, was issued many patents, and subsequently developed a line of hot-plate welding equipment called Hydra Sealer. By the mid-1980s, Tape Inc. and its Hydra Sealer division employed about 135 people. But Newkirk was starting to feel, in his words, "burnt out." In 1987, at the age of forty-five, he sold his company and retired to Arizona with plans to study photography and become a wildlife photographer. Two years later, Dunwoody recognized his achievements with its Alumni Entrepreneur Award.

But the retirement didn't last. After several years away from the manufacturing world, Newkirk gave in to his opportunistic nature and started looking for a way to get back into manufacturing. In 1993, he bought into a plastic injection molding business in Forest Lake that was soon renamed Teamvantage. A few years later, he bought out his partners and became the company's sole owner. Then, in 2003, another opportunity presented itself. Custom Mold & Design (CMD), a venerable manufacturer of precision molds founded by Dunwoody alum Duane Treiber, had fallen on hard times since being sold by Treiber to another firm. Newkirk, recognizing CMD's reputation and expertise, bought it and started

"The harder you work, the luckier you get."

—Ray Newkirk

building it back up. Fourteen years later, he acquired a third company, a mold design and manufacturing firm called Paradigme Engineering, owned by another Dunwoody alum, Jon Palmquist. By that time, Newkirk's post-retirement career had already lasted several years longer than his tenure at Tape Inc. and Hydra Sealer. Then, at age seventy-eight, he started thinking about stepping away. In 2020, he sold his three companies to an investment group, which then placed them under a single corporate umbrella called Velosity. He was retired again—sort of. "I've still got a key, and a little piece of the action," he said with a smile. "I pop in and out every now and then."

During a long career of starting, acquiring, and building up companies—not to mention helping to develop a certain bugle-shaped snack—Newkirk had repeatedly proven he was willing to act decisively when opportunities arose. And by his reckoning, his education at Dunwoody had a lot to do with that. He showed his appreciation, in part, by serving as a trustee of the College from 1999 through 2011. "We learned self-confidence and self-discipline," he said, looking back on his Dunwoody education. "Instructors were always pushing us to learn new things, even if sometimes difficult, and once you learned them, you left thinking, 'Hey, if I can do this, I can do anything!'"

DALE NORDQUIST

Electronic Systems Technology, 1974

It was 1982, the very beginning of the personal computer revolution, and Dale Nordquist had a big idea. The company he worked for, a Victoria, Minnesota–based manufacturer called HEI Inc., made and marketed light pens, a new class of interactive devices that made selections directly on computer screens. But Nordquist saw possibilities beyond pen-shaped pointers. He thought HEI should move into the market for a related product that had yet to take hold in the industry: the personal computer mouse. In a business plan produced after several months of research, Nordquist proposed that the company "seriously look at the mouse as a new product." The technology was "well within our capabilities," he argued, and while the mouse was available on the Xerox Star workstation, it was not yet produced for the personal computer market.

Nordquist's bosses looked over his proposal and issued their verdict: No.

"They said it probably would never become anything significant," he recalled later with a chuckle.

The mouse, of course, went on to become the computer world's dominant point-and-click device when, in 1984, Apple introduced it on the Macintosh computer. Nordquist filed away his proposal as an opportunity missed. But the episode demonstrated something important about him: a knack for seeing new opportunities and a vision for new corporate directions.

Nordquist had grown up on a dairy farm in northwestern Wisconsin, learning how to make and fix things. In 1972, he enrolled at Dunwoody, determined to put his mechanical aptitude to work. Two years later, he completed his training in Electronic Systems Technology, and started a long career that would take him in many unexpected directions. His first couple

Dale Nordquist with a few of his circuit boards.

jobs were service and sales positions, first with the film and photographic supply company Eastman Kodak, and then with American Sign and Indicator, a manufacturer of bank time-and-temperature signs and stadium scoreboards. (Among his biggest deals: the original scoreboard for Minneapolis's Metrodome, a $2 million project that included one of the first large-scale graphic displays for animation.) In 1981, he accepted a senior sales and marketing position with HEI, and entered what he would later call the "wide-open frontier" of high tech and rapidly advancing electronics.

Nordquist's unsuccessful attempt to nudge HEI into the computer mouse market did not affect his rise within the company. In the years that followed, and still at a young age, he took on increasingly senior positions with the now public company. He played key roles in a series of corporate reorganizations: the company's splitting into three divisions; its subsequent reintegration; and high-risk but successful moves into new worldwide markets for hearing aids, fiber optic communications, and disk drives. At each step along the way, he picked up skills that he would eventually put to use in the next stage of his career—of turning around struggling companies. "I was comfortable having lived through several reorganizations at HEI," he said. "I had confidence in myself and could handle the stress."

In 1999, after eighteen years at HEI, Nordquist took an ownership position in an underperforming company that made clean-room conveyors for semiconductor and disk drive manufacturing. After strategically repositioning that company, returning it to profitability, and overseeing its merger into another firm, he then moved to another stressed

"If something's messed up, I can't make it any worse. I can only make it better."

—Dale Nordquist

manufacturer—this one specializing in the assembly of custom circuit boards. While there, he led a strategic repositioning into new markets and the design and build of not just circuit boards but complete products. After that, he moved to yet another struggling firm, where he refocused its energies on its core business—the manufacture of energizers and insulators for electric fences. And finally, in 2010, he took over as president and CEO of GEOTEK, a manufacturer of fiberglass crossarms for electric utility poles. Unlike the other companies he had previously led in turnarounds, GEOTEK was a small, profitable manufacturer looking to scale up to the size that its owner, the private equity firm Granite Partners, envisioned. In Nordquist's six years there, GEOTEK grew from a $15 million company into a $50 million company. After that, he continued to serve as the board chair of both GEOTEK and another Granite Partners subsidiary, All Flex Solutions.

It hadn't ever occurred to Nordquist during his time at Dunwoody that his training in electronics would prepare him for the rigors of turning imminent corporate failures into unlikely success stories. But with the benefit of hindsight, it all made sense. He had come to Dunwoody in large part because of its dedication to the concept of learning by doing—and learning by fixing. The lessons he learned there had stuck. After all, he said, "if something's messed up, I can't make it any worse. I can only make it better."

ARTHUR POPEHN

Tool & Die, 1940

Not long after Art Popehn died in 2021, at the age of 101, E. J. Daigle, Academic Dean for Dunwoody's Robotics & Manufacturing, Computer Technology, Automotive, and Engineering departments, drove out to Plymouth to take a look at a gift Popehn had bequeathed to the College. The donation, a large collection of machinery and tools, was located in Popehn's home machine shop, and Daigle was prepared to be underwhelmed. But when the Dunwoody dean arrived, he realized he had stepped into someplace special. "It was a miniature Dunwoody," he said. Among the machines Popehn had acquired over the years was a mid-1980s Bridgeport mill in almost mint condition. "It obviously had been used," Daigle said, "but it was one of the best-maintained milling machines I had ever seen." Daigle arranged for the Bridgeport—and tens of thousands of dollars' worth of additional shop equipment—to make the move from Popehn's home to Dunwoody. The machine joined nineteen similar mills, all of them of more recent vintage, and it immediately stood out from the rest. "None of the others is in as good shape as this one is," Daigle said. "We're actually a little protective of it. You don't just get to jump on it and start whittling away at parts. You have to show us you know how to use it, and then we might let you on."

Art Popehn knew the value of a good machine, and he spent most of his 101 years around them. He had enrolled at Dunwoody during the late 1930s at the urging of a high school teacher who recognized his talent for taking things apart and putting them back together. After graduating from the school's Tool & Die program in 1940, and serving in the U.S. Navy during World War II, he went to work for a pair of local employers, Smith Welding and Honeywell. At the same time, he supplemented his income and satisfied his entrepreneurial urges by setting up a tool-and-die shop in the basement of the Minneapolis apartment building where he and his wife, Joanne, lived. During his off hours, he and a friend toiled away in the makeshift shop, doing small-scale stamping and tooling. They called their budding company Mid-Continent Engineering.

By the early 1950s, Mid-Continent had established itself as a reliable manufacturer of precision parts. Among its biggest clients was another World War II-era manufacturer, Minnesota Rubber and Gasket. In 1955, Popehn and his business partner put their expertise in making molds and inserts for the rubber industry to a new use. They created a subsidiary called Hiawatha Rubber, which quickly began building a reputation as a go-to manufacturer of high-tech, closely toleranced parts for the computer and printing markets. After nearly two decades with a pair of companies under his wings, Popehn sold Mid-Continent to focus his efforts on Hiawatha Rubber.

In the years that followed, Hiawatha continued to grow and prosper. Popehn ran the company until 1995, when he retired at the age of seventy-five, and handed the reins to his sons, Jim and Tom. But retirement was something of a misnomer where Popehn was concerned. He continued to show up at Hiawatha's manufacturing facility in Brooklyn Park into his nineties.

And all the while, he kept making things in that home workshop of his.

The Bridgeport and the other workshop gifts Popehn bequeathed to Dunwoody turned out to be fitting and functional memorials to a man who spent his life around machines. And that's probably just as Popehn would have wanted it. "There will always be a need for keeping the world going," he once said. "Everything is changing, and Dunwoody will change with it to produce the students the world needs."

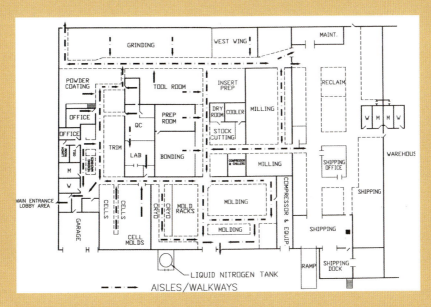

The floor plan of Hiawatha Rubber hinted at the extent of the company's operations.

"There will always be a need for keeping the world going. Everything is changing, and Dunwoody will change with it to produce the students the world needs."

—Arthur Popehn

BOB PORTER

Automotive Service Technology, 1970

It was the late 1960s. Bob Porter was a senior at Washburn High School, getting lousy grades, and living on his own in an apartment on Chicago Avenue so he could avoid what he would later describe as a "dysfunctional" family dynamic. The end of the school year was nearing, and he had no clue what graduation would bring. "I definitely was not college material," he admitted. Still, he did have two interests that he suspected might have the potential to determine his future: cars and money. As he tried to figure out how best to pursue a career focused on the former, he set to work on the latter. He had heard about a local investment firm called IDS, and he was intrigued. Unaware that seventeen-year-olds with few immediate prospects were typically considered dubious investor material, he called IDS to make an appointment. Not long after that, two investment advisors dressed in black suits, white shirts, and ties arrived at his little apartment on Chicago Avenue. "I was surprised they even came," he said. By the time they left, he was signed up to invest $25 a month in a mutual fund. Porter believed he had taken an important first step toward his future.

His mother did not.

"She got really mad," he said. "She thought they were scamming me."

Once Porter's mother got over what she considered her son's lapse in financial judgment (she had no way of knowing that, six years later, he would use the proceeds from his investments to buy his first home), she steered him in the direction of his other interest: automobiles. "I enjoyed working on cars," Porter said. "My mom recognized that. She said, 'You know, Bob, there's a place downtown called Dunwoody.' I had never heard of it." As he soon learned, his grandfather and great-uncle had both taught at the school, and a few other relatives had attended. After initially disavowing all interest in "trade school," he

Bob Porter and one of the perks of his four decades in financial management.

eventually had a change of heart. "The Vietnam War came, and it was either be in school or be drafted," he said. "So, I enrolled at Dunwoody."

During his two years in Dunwoody's Automotive program, Porter discovered that he was actually a good student. With his degree in hand, he quickly landed mechanic positions at a succession of local car dealerships. But even as he honed his automotive skills, he never shook his interest in business and finance. While continuing his garage work, he enrolled at Normandale Community College in Bloomington, thinking he might become an engineer. But repeated losing battles with calculus convinced him to reconsider his plans. He switched to business and discovered what he believed was his true calling. After two years at Normandale, he transferred into what was then called the College of Business Administration (later the Carlson School of Management) at the University of Minnesota. In 1974, he graduated from the U of M with a degree in accounting.

Porter's first job in his new career was a general accounting position. After that, he moved into auditing: three years with Carlson Companies, followed by eleven years with Gelco, a fleet-leasing firm. When his wife, Colleen, was transferred out of state by her employer, Cargill, he quit his job at Gelco and moved with her. From there, his career took multiple turns. He passed his Certified Public Accounting exam on his first try, ran a zinc oxide plant, took a technology firm public, and spent a couple years cleaning up the books of a struggling medical device company. After more than four decades in financial management, he retired in 2016.

With the benefit of hindsight, Porter recognized that he had planted at least some of the seeds of his success many years earlier, as a teenager, when he pursued his dual interests in making money and working on cars. He had scratched the first itch by investing $25 a month in an IDS mutual fund. He had relieved the second one by enrolling at Dunwoody. And while he didn't wind up making a career in auto repair, he never regretted his Dunwoody decision, and he never hesitated to recommend the school to others. "You're going to graduate from Dunwoody knowing that there won't be many people better than you," he said. "You can't emphasize that enough."

"You're going to graduate from Dunwoody knowing that there won't be many people better than you. You can't emphasize that enough."

—Bob Porter

Morgan Potter (34) and his fellow Dunwoody faculty members, 1930s.

MORGAN POTTER

Automotive Service Technology, 1924

During the first day of qualifying at the 1959 Indianapolis 500, driver Tony Bettenhausen was taking his Ansted Rotary Special on a final practice run, circling the track at about 142 miles an hour, when he lost control coming out of the southeast turn. The car went into a spin, hit the inside guardrail nose-first, flipped over, and slid thirty-three feet upside down. Bettenhausen was shaken, but suffered only a cut nose. His car, however, was crumpled almost beyond recognition. It was, in the estimation of one sportswriter, "a washout."

Morgan Potter disagreed.

Potter was a nationally recognized expert in welding. He was a 1924 graduate of Dunwoody Institute, a longtime instructor in its Welding department, and the author of a widely used textbook titled *Oxyacetylene Welding*, which went through multiple printings. In 1937, after more than a decade at Dunwoody, he accepted a job as head of welding at Marquette Manufacturing, a Minneapolis maker of welding equipment and battery chargers. Within a couple years he was promoted to sales manager. It was in that role that he came to pass judgment on the condition of Tony Bettenhausen's mangled Ansted Rotary.

In 1948, Potter had helped Marquette land an exclusive twelve-year contract with the Indianapolis Speedway to provide welding services during the month leading up to and through the big race. In the time since then, Marquette and its technicians had earned a reputation for working magic at the racetrack. For example, in 1952, one of Potter's welders managed to keep driver Jimmy Reece in the race by repairing his car's split fuel tank with the fuel still inside—an act of welding wizardry that at least one observer called "suicidal." Potter was not shy about touting such accomplishments. "Frequently cars come to the speedway almost entirely disassembled," he explained. "They have been racing on dirt

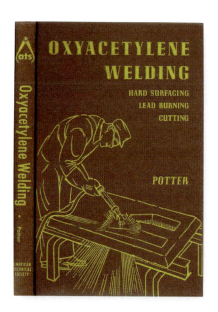

Morgan Potter wrote his textbook, *Oxyacetylene Welding*, after leaving Dunwoody's faculty.

tracks or asphalt and need to be rebuilt and toughened for the hard, rough brick surface at Indianapolis." It was Marquette's job, he said, to weld each car's pieces back together—whether it showed up at the Brickyard disassembled or fell apart while it was there.

When Bettenhausen wrecked his Ansted Rotary coming out of the speedway's southeast turn a couple weeks before the 1959 race, the members of Potter's Marquette crew suspected they might be called on to put the car back together—despite its dire condition. They were right. After a crew from another company straightened everything out, piece by piece, the Marquette team went to work. The car was restored. Potter contacted *Minneapolis Tribune* sportswriter Dick Cullum to make sure his people got proper credit. "The pieces have been put together by countless welds," Cullum reported after taking Potter's call, "and the car is back on the track, ready for its time trial."

The publicity Potter generated for Marquette Manufacturing through its relationship with the Indianapolis 500 raised the company's profile and helped solidify its reputation for making high-quality equipment used in garages throughout the United States and around the world. It was a marketing coup in which he probably took great pride. After all, Potter considered himself first and foremost a salesman, even if he initially made his name as a welder and instructor at Dunwoody. As a cultivator of relationships, Potter joined and promoted multiple professional and trade organizations—including Dunwoody's early Alumni Association—

and maintained those memberships throughout his career. His enthusiasm rarely wavered, and sometimes got the best of him. Such was the case in 1960, when he spoke at a conference of Utah sales executives. In making a point about the nurturing of sales teams, he employed an analogy that probably made at least a few listeners shake their heads in amusement. "The upgrading of salesmen is a subject that is dear to my heart and is tied directly to your and to my own purse strings," he proclaimed. "We, as sales executives, are the alchemists and the cavemen of a thousand years ago, because, as we face the present, we have the same challenges—of converting common clay into 'gold' and harnessing the power of man."

A 1924 graduate and longtime instructor in the Welding department, Morgan Potter was instrumental in helping Marquette Manufacturing land an exclusive contract with the Indianapolis Speedway.

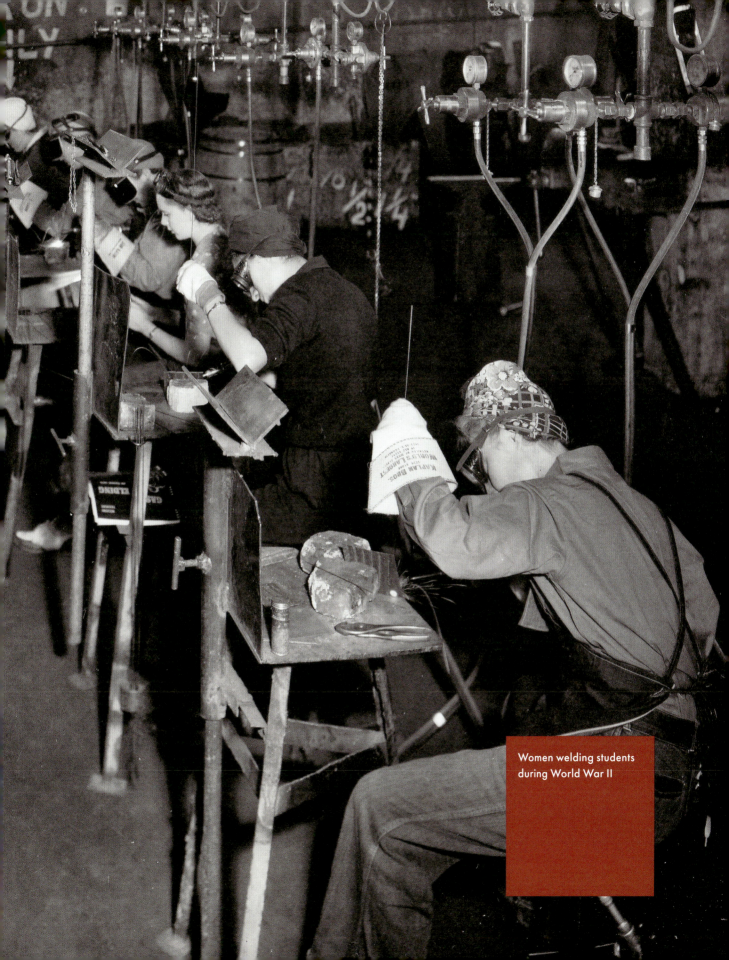

Women welding students during World War II

LARRY RAASCH

Architectural Drafting & Estimating, 1977

It's not often that a young student from New Orleans chooses to head north and enroll at Dunwoody, but in Larry Raasch's case, the decision seemed almost preordained. Raasch had spent the first few years of his life in the Chicago area, and then, at the age of six, had moved away along with the rest of his family when his father took a new job in Louisiana. The younger Raasch grew up in the South, and after graduating from high school, spent two years taking pre-engineering classes at the University of New Orleans. But then he heard the call of the North. His father was a Minnesota native, and he still had a lot of relatives there. One of them, a cousin named Steve Johnson, was enrolled in Dunwoody's Electrical program. During a visit to New Orleans, Johnson told Raasch all about the technical school he was attending in Minneapolis, and urged his cousin to consider enrolling. Raasch was already familiar with Dunwoody. He had heard about how his father had once hoped to attend the school, but abandoned that dream to serve in World War II. Now Raasch weighed the possibility of going there himself. "Dunwoody had a very stellar reputation," he later recalled. "I figured I'd give it a try."

Raasch moved back to Minnesota in 1975 and enrolled in Dunwoody's Architectural Drafting & Estimating program. After graduating two years later, he was hired as a draftsman by Fabcon, a Savage, Minnesota–based manufacturer of precast concrete. Raasch stayed with Fabcon for three years, rising to head of the drafting and estimating department, before accepting a project manager position with Kraus-Anderson, one of the Twin Cities' largest general contractors. It was, in essence, a move made possible by a mutual understanding between his old boss and his new boss. "The president of Fabcon and the president of Kraus were good friends," Raasch said. "They knew I had higher ambition."

Larry Raasch (bottom row, far right) and his fellow Architectural Drafting & Estimating graduates, 1977.

In the years that followed, Raasch worked on many of Kraus-Anderson's most notable projects, including construction of the Canterbury Downs horse racing track in Shakopee, Calhoun Square in Minneapolis's Uptown district, and a new library and a new science building at Augustana College in Rock Island, Illinois. He climbed the company's managerial ladder, eventually rising to vice president level. Twenty-five years after joining Kraus-Anderson, he decided to go into business for himself.

"I just wanted to do it," he said.

In 2005, Raasch and a fellow Dunwoody alum, Gregg Paschke, established Prime General Contractors LLC. The new company quickly made a name for itself as a successful midsize general contractor specializing in corporate, medical, and senior housing construction, with much of its work focused on the nonprofit sector. In 2019, after nearly fifteen years at Prime, Raasch retired, leaving the company in the hands of Paschke and yet another Dunwoody graduate, Derek Clarkin.

Looking back on his career, Raasch could see an almost uninterrupted connection to the school he'd left New Orleans to attend. During his years at Kraus-Anderson, he had overlapped with dozens of fellow alumni who worked as project managers at the company.

His successors at Prime General Contractors were Dunwoody grads as well. He had received a 2011 Alumni Achievement Award in recognition of his extensive volunteer work on behalf of the College, including the establishment of a scholarship program through which he and his wife, Diane, supported women in the construction industry. And then there was his family. By his count, he had at least eleven relatives who attended Dunwoody, among them: daughter Kristina (2008, Interior Design); son Kyle (2010, Electrical Construction Design & Management); cousin Wayne Swenson (1965, Electrical); cousin Frank Faschingbauer (1970, Electrical Construction); cousin Clarence Faschingbauer (1970, Refrigeration); cousin Dean Swenson (1971, Electrical Construction); cousin Steve Johnson (1973, Electrical); brother-in-law Larry Czarnecki (1975, Machine Tool); and nephew Brian Henrich (2013, Construction Management). Even if he had wanted to, Raasch could never have escaped his connections to the College. "At family reunions," he said, "we stand around and talk about Dunwoody."

"At family reunions, we stand around and talk about Dunwoody."

—Larry Raasch

Architectural Drafting & Estimating instruction, around the time Larry Raasch was a student.

Leon Rankin (bottom right) with fellow Dunwoody counselors
Ken Haagenson (top left) and Walter Cox (top right) and financial aid director
Gayle Basford (bottom left).

LEON RANKIN

Electrical Construction & Maintenance, 1963

It was 1959. Leon Rankin had recently moved up to Minneapolis from his home state of Mississippi, and was working at a foundry specializing in electrical tubing. During a break, he asked one of the company's assistant engineers where he had received his training. "He said he had graduated from Dunwoody Institute," Rankin recalled, "and suggested that if I was interested, I should go down and make an application." After thinking it over for a while, Rankin decided to apply for entrance into Dunwoody's Electrical program. There was just one problem: Rankin was Black, and Dunwoody had never produced a Black electrical graduate. Rankin's coworkers were skeptical.

"They thought I was kidding," he said. "It just made me a little more determined to try."

Rankin applied and was accepted into the Electrical program, but had to wait more than a year for a slot to open up. It didn't take him long after starting classes to realize he faced extra hurdles that his white classmates did not. "Even after I got into school, some of the instructors told me I'd never get into the trade," he said.

But he proved those instructors wrong.

After graduating in 1963, Rankin became the first Black student to enroll in the electrical apprenticeship program of Minneapolis Local 292. Four years later, he passed his master's license examination and started his own electrical contracting company, Rankin Electric.

Whatever success Rankin enjoyed as a trailblazing Black electrician was soon eclipsed by his work as an advocate for other members of the Twin Cities' growing African American community. In 1972, he joined the board of directors of the Minneapolis Urban League (MUL), and, with fellow activists like Ron Edwards, Nellie Stone Johnson, and Elmer Childress, turned the MUL into an organization known nationally for boldness and achievement. Edwards called him "one of the most successful and effective civil rights leaders in the State of Minnesota." As time went on, Rankin assumed additional leadership roles with a host of other civic organizations, including KMOJ Radio, Phyllis Wheatley Community Center, and Pillsbury United Communities. Later, he earned a graduate degree in counseling from St. Mary's University.

About two decades after graduating from Dunwoody, Rankin returned to the school as an instructor and part-time minority counselor. Convinced that too many students of color arrived on campus without the skills they needed to succeed, he set out to do something about it. In 1988, he joined with President Warren Phillips to create the Youth Career Awareness Program (YCAP), an initiative designed to help high school students meet the academic requirements of technical schools like Dunwoody. Recruited after completing ninth grade, YCAPers who finished the three-year program became eligible for Dunwoody scholarships. "We wanted to emphasize the importance of high school academics," Rankin said, "to make sure that kids are exposed to a wide range of technical occupations."

Over the next three decades, YCAP worked with more than two thousand students to provide opportunities for career exploration, education, mentorship, and scholarships for careers in technology. It also served as a model for the next-generation program that replaced it, an initiative called Pathways to Careers (P2C), which was designed to attract, train, and graduate underserved and under-represented high schoolers in Minneapolis. And those familiar with YCAP knew that its success was due largely to Leon Rankin. Two years after his death in 2015, Bill Jordan, Dunwoody's past director of facilities, summed up his former colleague's legacy. "Leon was a very humble man," he said. "A great thinker. Highly intelligent. He's looking down at [Dunwoody] right now. And he's happy. We both believed that Dunwoody could do this for this community."

The Youth Career Awareness Program (YCAP), which Leon Rankin helped establish, was a model for the next-generation program that replaced it, an initiative called Pathways to Careers (P2C).

"We wanted to emphasize the importance of high school academics, to make sure that kids are exposed to a wide range of technical occupations."

—Leon Rankin, on the creation of the Youth Career Awareness Program

Doug Schieffer (fourth from right) with Northland crew at a

DOUG SCHIEFFER

Architectural Drafting & Estimating, 1996

It was the mid-1990s, and Doug Schieffer was back in his hometown of Yankton after spending a lost year at the University of South Dakota. He was, to put it kindly, searching for some direction. As the son of the owner of a residential concrete and masonry firm, he was familiar with the construction business, but he wasn't sure whether he wanted to follow in his father's footsteps. Still, he suspected the trades might be a good fit, and a former shop teacher suggested he consider attending Dunwoody Institute in Minneapolis. When he ran into an old classmate, Jarret Hallvin, who had recently enrolled there for the winter semester, it seemed a coincidence too good to ignore. Schieffer got on the phone and called Dunwoody's admissions office. But the woman he spoke with told him he was out of luck; the incoming class was full. That's when Schieffer realized just how desperate he was to get on with his life. "I explained to her that I needed to get out of Yankton and go to Dunwoody," he recalled. "I told her if I don't go now, I'll never go." The admissions officer promised to see what she could do.

An hour later, she called back. Schieffer was in.

"That was really cool of her," he said.

While attending Dunwoody, Schieffer parlayed his limited experience with his father's company into a part-time job as an estimator with a large industrial concrete and masonry firm. ("I didn't know what the hell I was doing," he said. "I was just trying to figure it out.") After graduation, he accepted a full-time position with the same company. He was following in his father's footsteps after all—even if it was on the commercial side of the business rather than on the residential side.

Schieffer's employer eventually failed, but he continued to gain experience as an estimator and project manager with two additional firms. In 2003, he jumped at the chance to become part-owner of another Twin Cities–area company, Northland Concrete & Masonry. Northland was an established firm dating back to the 1960s, but it had plateaued, with annual revenues totaling about $18 million. Schieffer set out to expand the company's sights by investing in new equipment and hiring new people. Within five years, Northland's revenues had jumped to $80 million. After weathering a few tough years brought on by the 2008 financial crisis, the company resumed its upward trajectory.

Schieffer explained Northland's accelerating success as a result of several factors, including the hiring of "the best people," large investments in equipment, and a willingness to take significant risks. Also important: an underappreciated evolution in the construction business. Schieffer had bought into Northland at a time of significant change in the way most high-rise structures were built. Before then, most tall buildings were framed using structural steel. But the terrorist attacks of September 11, 2001, which brought down the twin towers of New York's World Trade Center, exposed some fatal flaws in the reliance on steel construction. Designers of high-rises started switching to "post-tensioned," cast-in-place concrete—floors, columns, walls, you name it—as a way to help their buildings withstand greater stress. This shift created new opportunities for subcontractors willing and able to develop expertise in structural concrete, and Schieffer, who had gained some experience in bidding on such projects earlier in his career, steered Northland in that direction. As time went on, the company's structural concrete work accounted for an increasingly significant portion of its business. "I don't think we have a competitor that does half as much volume as we do," Schieffer said. By the early 2020s, Northland's annual revenues had risen to more than $200 million, and nearly a third of that came from structural concrete work.

Schieffer hadn't learned much about high-rise construction during his time at Dunwoody, but he credited the school with setting him on a path that led him into that and other areas of expertise. "As far as developing my initial skill set, I don't think Dunwoody could have done a better job," he said. He also recognized that he might never have attended Dunwoody in the first place had it not been for that admissions officer who made an extra effort on his behalf. "She went and pulled some strings for me," Schieffer said with a laugh. "I guess everything happens for a reason."

"As far as developing my initial skill set, I don't think Dunwoody could have done a better job."

—Doug Schieffer

Frank Schochet shows his Insty-Prints equipment to a
group of visiting Japanese printers, 1975.

FRANK SCHOCHET

Printing & Graphics Technology, 1935

The modern fast-food franchise, with its pre-prepared ingredients and made-while-you-wait convenience, was just becoming a mainstay of the American cultural and commercial landscape when, in 1963, Frank Schochet had a bright idea: why not take the concepts that made fast food so popular and successful and apply them to the field he knew best—printing? Schochet had been printing everything from business cards to holiday greetings since the 1920s, when he set up an old, hand-operated press in the basement of his parents' home. While attending the University of Minnesota in 1933 and 1934, he honed his skills by taking evening classes in presswork and linotype at Dunwoody Institute. After finishing at Dunwoody, he acquired a half-interest in Manette, Inc., a commercial printing plant in North Minneapolis. A few years after that, he bought out his partner, and—with his wife, Freda, handling the books—established a new subsidiary, Schochet Press. Frank Schochet did well for himself during the 1950s, but he was never quite satisfied. "I had long felt there was a need for some kind of technique for getting the quality of regular printing at lower production cost," he would later recall. Then, in 1963, he went to a trade show in New York and got his first glimpse of some new, high-speed lithographic offset printing equipment that would make it possible to do small jobs at affordable prices—and in a matter of minutes. That's when he came up with the idea to create a new business, what he called the "hamburger complex" of the printing world.

He called the company Instant Printing Service.

Schochet moved his new business to a bigger facility in Minneapolis's North Loop and began advertising in local newspapers. "New! Revolutionary!" the ads proclaimed. "Low-cost instant printing from your type-written, printed, hand-lettered, or hand-drawn copy—while you wait!" Schochet was on to something. Customers flocked to the new company to have their circulars, bulletins, handbills, catalogs, and sales letters printed on the spot.

One of Frank Schochet's first Insty-Prints ads.

"We're the fast-food business of the printing industry," he said. "We can attract small jobs that can be done quickly and cheaply. A customer can walk into one of our shops and if the machine is available, he can get one hundred letterheads printed in less than ten minutes. Any color he wants, just so it's black." Within a couple years, Schochet had six locations in the Twin Cities, all of them operating under a new name, Insty-Prints. But then a friend in Washington, DC, suggested he think even bigger. "He said I had the best instant printing operation in the [Country]," Schochet recalled. "He put us into the franchise business."

The first Insty-Prints shop located beyond the Twin Cities opened in Washington in 1967. From there, the company's growth was phenomenal. The Insty-Prints logo, with its familiar wand-wielding wizard, began showing up around the Country and as far away as Canada, Puerto Rico, Israel, Japan, and Thailand. By 1981, Insty-Prints—still privately held—had twenty-one company-owned stores and 240 franchised units and was earning nearly $500,000 a year on revenues of $6 million. It probably would have grown even faster if Schochet, a product of the Great Depression, hadn't been so cautious about selling his concept to prospective franchisees. "I think my hardest job is to blow the stardust out of their eyes," he said, "to get across to them that this is a business like any other ... and you must pay attention to [manage] it and nourish it."

In 1983, Frank and Freda Schochet sold Insty-Prints to Minneapolis financier Irwin Jacobs and retired. "It was probably the smartest thing I ever did," Frank said looking back on the sale, "because I knew nothing about digital printing, which is essentially what's done today." Over the next two decades, the Schochets made it a priority to give substantial portions of the sale's proceeds to causes and institutions that were important to them—including Dunwoody. It was a way to show thanks for what they considered their good fortune. "I had no idea it would be this huge," Frank said in summing up his success with Insty-Prints. "I was just trying to find a way we could print and sell copies for profit."

"A customer can walk into one of our shops and if the machine is available, he can get one hundred letterheads printed in less than ten minutes. Any color he wants, just so it's black."

—Frank Schochet

Printing & Graphics
Technology class, 1977

JOHN SCHUMACHER

Baking, 1965

It may be hard to believe now, given the sheer number of terrific restaurants in the Twin Cities and elsewhere in Minnesota, but the Land of 10,000 Lakes has not always been known as a land of fine cuisine. For many years, going out to dinner in Minnesota meant enjoying relatively humble fare in dowdy, old-fashioned surroundings. Even Minneapolis, the most cosmopolitan of the State's big cities, boasted just a few restaurants—Charlie's, Harry's, Murray's, maybe a couple others—that sophisticates considered anything close to a match for the high-class eateries in New York, Chicago, and Los Angeles. The lack of refined dining options was even more pronounced outside the Twin Cities. That was Minnesota's dining reality for much of the twentieth century. And it certainly was the case in the mid-1970s, when John Schumacher bought and refurbished a seventy-eight-year-old hotel in New Prague, about an hour's drive southwest of the Twin Cities, and turned part of it into a restaurant. He had an audacious plan to bring fine cuisine to greater Minnesota.

The folks in town just "looked on and chuckled," he said.

Schumacher had grown up in rural Wheaton, Minnesota, and after high school had fled to Minneapolis to get "out from behind the cows" and enroll in Dunwoody's Baking program. After graduating in 1965 (quite an accomplishment, since dyslexia made it almost impossible for him to read), he served in the U.S. Navy as a baker and cook aboard nuclear submarines. From there, he went to New Haven, Connecticut, to train at the Culinary Institute of America. That led to executive chef positions with Marriott hotels in Washington, DC, and Bloomington, Minnesota. By the early 1970s, he was itching to be his own boss.

It took Schumacher and his first wife about three years to refurbish the old Hotel Broz after they purchased it in 1974. When Schumacher's New Prague Hotel finally opened in 1977, its restaurant was an almost instant hit. Inspired by New Prague's immigrant past,

Schumacher loaded his menu with Czech and German specialties. He made nearly everything from scratch—cut his own veal, pickled his own cucumbers, and sourced his flour from a local mill. Over time, word of his unlikely fine dining establishment spread well beyond southern Minnesota. National publications like *Bon Appétit*, *Better Homes & Gardens*, *Gourmet*, *Country Living*, and *USA Today* ran articles about him. With help from his second wife, he overcame his dyslexia to write *John Schumacher's New Prague Hotel Cookbook*, which went through several printings. Happy patrons periodically wrote their local newspapers for help in obtaining specific recipes, and he frequently obliged, as he did with this recipe for an old-world classic:

Czech Potato Dumplings

Potatoes to make 1 quart mashed

4 cups bread flour

1 teaspoon salt

1 egg, beaten

Boil, peel, and mash potatoes and place in large bowl. When cool, add flour, salt, and beaten egg. Mix by hand to thoroughly combine all ingredients. Shape into 3-ounce cylinder-shaped dumplings.

In pot, bring salted water to a fast boil. Place dumplings in the boiling water. Dumplings will fall to bottom of pot, so gently stir dumplings off the bottom. Bring water back to a fast boil for about 15 minutes. Check to see if fully cooked in the center. When fluffy and white all the way through, it is done. Remove dumplings from the water. Make a slit in the center of each dumpling and brush with butter.

"The first day [the restaurant] was open, I couldn't raise fifty dollars to put in the till to make change."

—John Schumacher

Schumacher operated the restaurant for nearly three decades before closing it in 2005. During that time and in the years that followed, he won numerous accolades, including an induction into the Minnesota Hospitality Hall of Fame and an Alumni Entrepreneur Award from Dunwoody. In a profile published in the school's alumni newsletter earlier in his career, the writer of the piece had urged fellow Dunwoody graduates to make the trek to New Prague to experience the excellent food, service, and atmosphere at Schumacher's place. "You'll be happy you made the trip," he wrote. "And say hello to John. He'll be happy to know you're a Dunwoody alum."

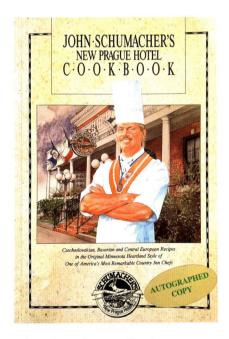

John Schumacher's cookbook was originally published in 1992.

MARK SHERRY

Architectural Drafting & Estimating, 1987

When his post-high-school plans for college fell through in 1982, Mark Sherry decided to try something completely different. He entered the trades, working as a carpenter, carpet layer, or whatever decent position he could land in the construction business. The work paid reasonably well, and he gained some useful skills. But after three years, he'd had enough. The final straw came one afternoon, after a particularly grueling day of deck building in Lakeville. "I couldn't have been more frustrated," he recalled. "I was hand-digging forty-two holes in dirt filled with rocks." On his way home, he drove past Dunwoody College—and then impulsively turned around. "I enjoy being spontaneous," he admitted. "It was just one of those moments. I walked to the desk and asked about the programs. They said, well, one's starting in two weeks." With those forty-two holes still fresh in his mind, Sherry enrolled in Dunwoody's Architectural Drafting & Estimating program.

Sherry started at Dunwoody with the ultimate goal of becoming an architect, but he soon discovered that he preferred getting out of the office and into the field. He particularly enjoyed commercial construction. During his second year at the school, he landed a part-time job as an estimator with Mortenson Construction. After graduation, he slid smoothly into a full-time position with the company.

As it turned out, Sherry launched his Mortenson career at an auspicious moment. The company had recently landed its first major public construction project—the new Minneapolis Convention Center—and Sherry found himself working up estimates for various portions of that job. Before long, he was working on even bigger projects—both local and national—including a major expansion of the Los Angeles Convention Center, designed by world-renowned architect I. M. Pei.

The Los Angeles Convention Center, after its expansion, on which Mark Sherry and his Mortenson colleagues successfully bid.

The bidding for the Los Angeles project proved to Sherry that, under the right circumstances, estimating could generate heart-pounding excitement. In a scene reminiscent of a Hollywood thriller, Sherry and a few dozen colleagues set up shop in a hotel conference room and waited until the last possible moment to call in their bid to a pair of runners at the county courthouse. With the clock ticking down, the Mortenson runners raced up two floors, through an active movie production, and delivered the bid. (One of Mortenson's three competitors failed to get past the film crew in time, and was disqualified.) A few minutes later, Sherry and his Mortenson colleagues got the call they'd been hoping for. Their bid of $287 million was the lowest. They won the job.

"We had cocktails brought to the conference room," Sherry said. "It was so much fun."

As the years went by, the fun (along with the occasional not-so-fun) continued. Sherry moved up the estimating ladder at Mortenson, played a key role in establishing the company's successful Milwaukee office, and was eventually promoted into the executive ranks, where he took over responsibility for the company's burgeoning wind energy and real estate operations. Along the way, he became a strong advocate for bringing more people into the trades. Among the initiatives he and Mortenson championed was Dunwoody's Pathways to Careers program, which awarded substantial scholarships to underserved and under-represented individuals pursuing construction degrees at Dunwoody. Sherry hoped other construction firms would eventually join Mortenson in supporting the effort. "We all need people right now," he said. "If we and others can create opportunities for those who might not otherwise have access to a Dunwoody education, then that's a gift that will give a return for their entire careers."

When Sherry touted the return on investment that a Dunwoody education could provide, he spoke from personal experience. "The decision I made in 1985 to pull into the parking lot at Dunwoody and sign up for its Drafting & Estimating program was the best decision I ever made," he said. "I couldn't be happier about the value that my Dunwoody education provided to me."

"The decision I made in 1985 to pull into the parking lot at Dunwoody and sign up for its Drafting & Estimating program was the best decision I ever made."

—Mark Sherry

HOWARD SIEWERT

Printing & Graphics Technology, 1956

Back in the 1950s, when Howard Siewert was taking printing classes at Dunwoody, training to become a printer often meant learning how to operate a linotype machine. At the time, linotype was state-of-the-art technology in the printing world. Linotype machines were hulking metal contraptions about the size and weight of an automobile, loud, dirty, and smelly. But they couldn't operate on their own. They required the efforts of trained typesetters—often dressed in stained leather aprons—who punched letters and spaces on a special keyboard and set in motion a process resulting in a line of type, also known as a slug, made of cooled molten lead. Those slugs were then bunched together into paragraphs and sent off to presses that printed newspapers, magazines, and posters. Dunwoody was a leader in training linotype operators, and Siewert graduated from the program well prepared. His first job out of school was with a newspaper in Stewartville, Minnesota. But after two years there, the big machines he had been trained to operate no longer held much appeal. "I didn't want to be a linotype operator for the rest of my life," he said. Siewert started looking for other options, and it was a good thing he did. Over the next decade-plus, linotype would become completely obsolete.

Siewert moved back to the Twin Cities and took some classes at the University of Minnesota, but money was tight, and he ended up accepting a new job with a small printing company in South Minneapolis. He still had to do some linotype work, but gradually he took on other types of jobs. Eventually, he moved into the front of the shop, working directly with customers. While there, he enrolled in a night course at Dunwoody to learn estimating. With his additional training, he then landed a job as an estimator with McGill Graphic Arts, one of the Twin Cities' biggest printing companies. His tenure at McGill lasted fourteen years, including a five-year stint as general manager. From there, he moved to a sales position with a nationally known printer based in Waseca, Minnesota, where he managed accounts worth hundreds of thousands of dollars. After five years there, he quit.

"I didn't have a game plan," he admitted.

By that point, a lot had changed in the years since Siewert graduated from Dunwoody. The linotype machine on which he trained had been displaced by new technology. He had turned himself from a technician into a successful estimator and salesman. But the stress of working with big catalog and publishing clients in Chicago and on the East Coast had taken a toll. "I thought I'd rather work in a small place," he said, "work for myself." In 1979, he and his wife, Rhoda, bought a small printing company in North Minneapolis and renamed it Ideal Printers. "It was quite a departure, walking up and down Broadway selling business cards and office forms," he recalled. "But I found that I got a lot of satisfaction working for small companies and doing a good job for them."

Ideal started with four or five employees and grew from there. The company moved into successively larger facilities, first in St. Paul's Midway area and later on the east edge of downtown. Its workforce doubled and doubled and doubled again. When the Siewerts finally retired during the late 1990s, their daughters Lana and Joan took over, maintaining Ideal's status as a family-owned-and-operated business. From his vantage as the company's owner emeritus, Howard Siewert could see that his training had been made obsolete by technological advances in the printing industry, but he continued to value his Dunwoody education—even if it was a bit linotype-heavy. "It proved," he said, "to be a wonderful base on which to build."

"We never had a plan in writing. We just did what seemed like the right thing to do, always with the intention of growing."

—Howard Siewert

Example of the kind of linotype machine Howard Siewert worked with early in his career.

Harold Slawik accepts the 1960 Twin Cities Ford
Dealer of the Year Award.

HAROLD SLAWIK

Automotive Repair, 1916

These days, if you're looking to buy a new car in the Twin Cities area, you probably will end up at a dealership on one of several strips in the suburbs—maybe along I-394 in Minnetonka, I-494 in Bloomington, I-35W in Burnsville, or Highway 61 in White Bear Lake. The selling and purchasing of new automobiles has, over the past few decades, become a mostly suburban proposition. But there was a time, not so long ago, when people in Minneapolis and St. Paul—and even the suburbs—shopped for cars almost exclusively within the city limits. And no Twin Cities car-buying destination was more popular than St. Paul's University Avenue.

University first became identified with the automobile during the 1910s, when the Ford Motor Company and its rival, Willys-Overland, built manufacturing plants on opposite ends of the avenue. (Dunwoody Institute operated an aircraft mechanic training school in the Willys-Overland complex during World War I.) But in the 1920s, University Avenue began to attract the area's largest concentration of car dealerships. One of the strip's earliest and most successful dealers was a 1916 alumnus of Dunwoody named Harold Slawik.

Slawik was the son of German immigrants, and his father was a respected fur merchant in St. Paul. Born in 1901, Harold demonstrated from an early age that he had an aptitude for business and salesmanship. As a teen, he operated a bicycle repair shop out of his family's home on Marshall Avenue. It was during that early entrepreneurial period that he attended Dunwoody. At some point after finishing his Dunwoody education, he graduated from bicycle repair to auto repair. Eventually, he started selling cars in addition to fixing them. By the early 1930s, Slawik was operating a Plymouth and DeSoto (a division of Chrysler) dealership in downtown St. Paul. Within a few years, he moved his entire operation, now known as Slawik Motors, to a new location on University Avenue.

DE SOTO - PLYMOUTH

Guaranteed Reconditioned Used Cars

We Have for Your Approval 90 Used Cars

All Prices, Makes and Models

We Invite Your Inspection

HAROLD J. SLAWIK

Main at 7 Corners   CEdar 3644

Harold Slawik's first car dealership was located in downtown St. Paul.

World War II brought Slawik's new car business to a halt, and he spent much of the war managing the Twin Cities district of the Office of Price Administration (OPA), the agency that, among other things, oversaw the rationing of food and other goods. When the war ended and his work with OPA was complete, he went back to selling cars. Slawik stayed with Plymouth and DeSoto for a while, but eventually, he switched to Ford. His new dealership, Midway Ford, continued to anchor the southwest corner of University and Fairview, and was known for displaying its latest models on a tall outdoor pedestal that looked something like an oversized martini glass.

Not satisfied to limit himself to the selling of cars, Slawik and his business partner wife, Marie, moved into real estate development. They saw particularly exciting opportunities for growth in the inner-ring suburb of Roseville, and began investing there. In 1961, they broke ground on a new shopping mall at a busy intersection on Snelling Avenue. But while the mall was under construction, Harold died, leaving Marie to oversee the project's completion. The new shopping center, called Har Mar (a mashup of the first three letters of the Slawiks' two first names) opened in 1962. Marie continued to run the family's varied business, and in 1977, she moved Midway Ford to a new location in Roseville, about a mile north of Har Mar, where it continues to operate today.

Harold Slawik's connection to Dunwoody faded over the years, but there's little doubt he considered his time there pivotal. A 1937 edition of the *Dunwoody News* noted that Slawik, "in remembrance of his Dunwoody school days," had recently donated five automobiles to the school so that a younger generation of students could receive the kind of hands-on training that helped make him successful. The piece included a not-so-subtle pitch to graduates of the school's Automobile Mechanics program. "Anyone interested in [auto] work would do well to pay a visit to Mr. Slawik's place of business," the article concluded. "You will always find a hearty welcome at Harold Slawik's."

"Anyone interested in [auto] work would do well to pay a visit to Mr. Slawik's place of business. You will always find a hearty welcome at Harold Slawik's."

—*Dunwoody News*, February 19, 1937

World War I Army
training

STEVE STONE

Electrical Construction & Maintenance, 1977

When Steve Stone graduated from high school in 1974, his plans for the future were, to put it kindly, unformulated. "I didn't have any idea what I wanted to do," he admitted. Still, he didn't lack for family role models when it came to choosing a career path for himself. His grandfather William was a house painter, handyman, and prolific artist known for landscapes of prominent Twin Cities and family locations. His uncle Russell was an HVAC installer with Fred Vogt & Co. His father, Billy, was an electrician with Cramer Electric and Control Data Corp. And all three of them were Dunwoody graduates. Stone had never felt pressured by any of his Dunwoody-alum relatives to follow in their footsteps, but he admired what they all had accomplished during their careers. He was particularly impressed with his father, who took pride in his education and seemed to genuinely enjoy heading off to work each morning in his Cramer Electric Co. service truck. After thinking it over, Stone enrolled in Dunwoody's Electrical Construction & Maintenance program, and then shared the news with his dad. "I can still picture his face," he recalled. "'Holy cow!' he said. 'You did? Really?' He was pretty proud. So were my grandfather and my uncle."

Stone graduated from Dunwoody in 1977, intent on becoming a field electrician, just like his father. He was accepted into the local electrical apprenticeship program, and over the next three years worked for three contractors specializing in three different types of construction: residential, commercial, and industrial. At the end of those three years, Stone passed his journeyman's test and was hired as a foreman at Loop Belden Porter, the industrial firm where he'd been working as an apprentice. He was now a journeyman and master electrician going from job to job in his own service truck—just like his father. "Out in the field," he said. "That's where I liked to be."

But it's not where he ended up.

The first generation of Stone family Dunwoody graduates (left to right): Billy Stone (1955, Electrical Construction & Maintenance); Russell Stone (1949, Sheet Metal); and William Stone (1940, Painting & Papering).

In 1983, Loop Belden Porter's electrical division was purchased by another local contractor, Parsons Electric. Stone continued working for a while as a field electrician, driving one of Parsons' signature black and white service vans, but his bosses eventually asked him to move behind a desk. Thus began a thirty-two-year rise through the company's ranks. In 1985, he became the general superintendent overseeing all Parsons service work. A few years later, he moved into project management. In 1998, he was named vice president in charge of the company's service and special projects group. And the following year, after the private equity firm that acquired the company failed, he became co-owner and partner. Over the next fifteen years, until his retirement in 2015, he continued on in that role, and helped build Parsons into one of the Twin Cities' most successful electrical contracting companies. "Not by any stretch of the imagination did I ever think that would eventually happen," he said, looking back on his rise from journeyman to executive.

Stone had gotten his start in the business by enrolling at Dunwoody, the same school his father, uncle, and grandfather had attended. They had all taken pride in seeing him follow their examples. But the Stone family's Dunwoody connection did not end there. In 1999, the same year Steve Stone became part-owner of Parsons, his son Corey enrolled at Dunwoody and started down a path that would lead to a Bachelor of Architecture degree and a career in building information modeling. That made four generations of Stones with degrees from Dunwoody, a rare, unbroken line: father, son, grandson, and great-grandson—not to mention uncle. And Steve Stone honored that connection through two decades of volunteer work with the Dunwoody Alumni Association Board, including two years as president. "I honestly don't think I'd be where I am today without my Dunwoody degree," he said. "And it's definitely a source of pride that so many of my family have gone there."

"I honestly don't think I'd be where I am today without my Dunwoody degree."

—Steve Stone

Vern Taaffe

VERN TAAFFE

NEI, 1977

Back in the 1970s, dialysis—a mechanized process that filters waste products and excess fluid from the blood of people whose kidneys have stopped working properly—was still in its infancy. The basic procedure had been developed decades earlier, but the technology was still relatively crude. At the same time, the number of Americans diagnosed with what would later be known as chronic kidney disease was on the verge of exploding, driven largely by rising rates of diabetes, high blood pressure, and obesity. Demand for new and improved methods of dialysis—and the equipment it required—was beginning to grow, and a handful of startup companies were gearing up to respond.

This was the world in which Vern Taaffe chose to make his career.

A native of South Minneapolis, Taaffe had developed an early interest in machinery (as a teenager, he repaired electromechanical pinsetters at a local bowling alley) and auto mechanics. After graduating from high school, he was accepted into a mechanical engineering program at the Twin Cities location of what was then known as General Motors Institute (GMI), under the sponsorship of a local Oldsmobile dealership, where he worked as an apprentice auto technician. Within four years, he had earned his GMI degree and certification as a journeyman auto technician.

And he might have kept working there indefinitely had he not been laid off in the midst of a nationwide economic downturn. The experience convinced him to look for a new career. Having developed an interest in electronics while working at the dealership, he enrolled in a continuous two-year program at Northwestern Electronics Institute (NEI), a Minneapolis technical college that would later merge with Dunwoody. After graduating with honors and the equivalent of more than two hundred college credits in engineering, he received five job offers. The one that most intrigued him came from a dialysis products startup called Renal

Systems. "I took a hard look at it," he said, "because it involved hydraulics, mechanics, electronics, chemistry, and microbiology—all those disciplines. And I said to myself, this is a place where I can contribute, grow, learn, and do well."

Taaffe went to work at Renal Systems in 1977, as a research and development engineer. Over the next fourteen years, he played crucial roles in the design and development of some of the company's most successful products, including blood pumps, conductivity meters, air detectors, and concentrate manufacturing systems. Perhaps his biggest success came with his participation in the design and development of what was known in the industry as a dialyzer reprocessing system—essentially a machine that flushed, cleaned, tested, and dispensed sterilant solution into artificial kidneys used in dialysis. While there, he developed additional expertise by working closely with Ph.D.'s in chemistry and microbiology, and by attending dozens of workshops. His commitment to continuing education became an enduring and defining feature of his career.

In 1991, Taaffe left what was then known as Minntech Corporation to start two companies of his own. Reprocessing Products Corporation (RPC) focused on providing products for, and improving dialyzer reprocessing within, dialysis clinics. Rabrenco Scientific manufactured products, like test strips, blood pressure cuffs, and dialysate sample ports that helped ensure patient safety during the typical four-hour dialysis process. Four years after founding the two companies, Taaffe merged them into a single firm under the RPC umbrella. The newly consolidated RPC had manufacturing facilities in Minneapolis and Tucson, Arizona.

Unlike other companies with diversified product lines, RPC kept its focus exclusively on kidney dialysis. As the demand for dialysis grew and dialysis providers realized the unique user and patient benefits of RPC's products, Taaffe's company came to dominate its segment of the industry. Taaffe became a widely recognized speaker and presenter at national dialysis workshops and symposiums, and served on a variety of standards boards. Ultimately, the National Association of Nephrology Technologists (NANT) presented him with its highest honor, the NANT President's Award.

Although Taaffe never actually attended Dunwoody, the course of study he completed at NEI continued, in updated form, in Dunwoody's Electronics Engineering Technology program—a program that offered the type of technical training he considered essential, whether it came in *preparation* for a career or *during* it. "Virtually everything today has some technical tie to it," he said. "Technical education is important now, but it will be more and more important as we move forward into the future."

"Technical education is important now, but it will be more and more important as we move forward into the future."

—Vern Taaffe

Ray Thelen was among Dunwoody's 1940 baking graduates.

RAY THELEN

Baking, 1940

In 1975, a Dunwoody Baking program graduate named Ray Thelen self-published a unique cookbook titled *Everything You Need to Know about Cookies: How to Create Them, Make Them, Bake Them*. To the uninitiated, the publication of another book of cookie recipes might have seemed like overkill. But Thelen didn't write his cookbook for the average home-kitchen cookie maker. His target readers were commercial bakers, the owners and operators of small-to-medium-sized shops who were looking to succeed in business. His goal, he wrote, was to help bakeries "produce top-quality, consumer-satisfying cookies for a more profitable cookie operation." In his opinion, success in the cookie field depended on four things: superior ingredients, well-balanced recipes, proper equipment, and controlled processing—and there was no room for compromise on any of those essentials.

> Are not some of us showing the [wrong] attitude toward our customers when it comes to giving a "full measure?" Are we really trying to give them what they want and expect from us, or do we just give them what is easy, convenient, and economical for us to make, and then expect them to accept it and be satisfied? If our sales are not exactly what we would like or expect them to be, then perhaps we are guilty of compromise.

Thelen had reason to believe there would be a market for his book. Over the course of his career, he had become one of the baking industry's most knowledgeable and respected researchers and teachers. If anyone knew what it took to make a successful cookie operation, it was him.

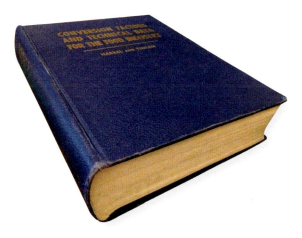

Ray Thelen's first book, *Conversion Factors and Technical Data for the Food Industry,* was a bit longer and heavier than his follow-up, *Everything You Need to Know about Cookies.*

Thelen claimed he had spent all but the first eight years of his life in the baking business. In his first job at the Sunlight Bakery in his hometown of St. Cloud, he performed mostly menial tasks like sweeping floors and cleaning and greasing pans. But as he entered his teens, he picked up more and more tricks of the trade while working at a succession of retail and wholesale bakeries.

He enrolled in Dunwoody's Baking program, and upon graduation in 1940, took a job as a "soft wheat test baker" at the Pillsbury Company in Minneapolis. The position required him to head out into the field, solving what he called "flour-related baking problems." It was the first step in becoming a baking technology troubleshooter and communicator.

In the years that followed, Thelen spent a growing proportion of his time as an on-site consultant for clients servicing the baking industry. In 1966, he joined Mother Murphy's Laboratories, a North Carolina–based flavoring company with which he remained associated for the rest of his career. But even while he was with Mother Murphy's, he continued his independent consulting work. Industry insiders came to think of him as an invaluable resource. He could be counted on to offer a professional opinion, based on thorough research, when asked to weigh in on the pros and cons of changing a product's ingredients. He traveled the Country doing seminars, offering one-on-one guidance, and teaching classes at institutions like the American Institute of Baking, where he served as guest lecturer and demonstrator. He also wrote for a variety of trade publications, including *Bakers' Helper*, which ran his popular "Ask Ray" column for many years.

When asked to provide his professional qualifications, Thelen often made a point of mentioning his alma mater. Dunwoody was, in fact, the only specific place—school, company, or otherwise—that he chose to include in the author's biography on the back cover of his *Cookies* book. When the American Society of Baking posthumously inducted him into its Baking Hall of Fame in 2006, it too made sure to mention his connection to Dunwoody—the place he went "to complete his education" in the field he loved.

"For you, the baker, to realize a successful cookie operation, you must never consider a compromise."

—Ray Thelen

DUANE TREIBER

Machine Tool Technology, 1958

Duane Treiber was eight or nine years old, growing up on his family's farm in Hebron, North Dakota, when he came across a book he would later describe as "the greatest inspiration" of his life. *Forty Power Tools You Can Make* was a publication of *Popular Mechanics* magazine, a how-to guide that found wide readership during the rationing and scrap drive years of World War II. From an early age, Treiber had displayed an aptitude for building highly detailed miniature models of ships, airplanes, and cars. Now he had an instruction manual on how to build something bigger—and potentially more useful. With visions of grinders, lathes, and sanders dancing in his head, he became a regular browser at the junkyard across the street from the creamery that bought the milk produced by his family's thirty dairy cows. He built his first machine power tool, a drill press, using a mishmash of salvaged parts, including connecting rods from a car and a hand brake from an old truck. After that came other homemade power tools that he considered necessary additions to a functioning shop: a snag grinder, a horizontal milling machine, a more capable, heavy-duty drill press. To hone his skills (and keep his ever-skeptical father at bay), he started building junkyard contraptions designed to make life on the farm easier: a straw bale spreader, a grain auger, a walk-behind garden tractor.

After graduating from high school, marrying, and working for a few years both as a farmer and as a part-time auto mechanic, Treiber decided once and for all that he was not cut out for a life on the farm. "The mechanical part was challenging," he explained. "I just did not care for the livestock part." Determined to turn his fascination with machines into a full-time career, he enrolled at Dunwoody Institute, the only school he could find that offered the kind of toolmaking courses he was looking for. He and his wife, Shirley, packed up their

The book that changed Duane Treiber's life.

old Pontiac and moved to Minneapolis. For the better part of two years, he took classes at Dunwoody and paid his way by working part-time in the school's maintenance department.

It was "machine heaven," he said.

Treiber's first job out of school was, in his words, "interesting," but it didn't give him much chance to put his toolmaking skills to work. Eventually, he landed a job more to his liking at Booker & Wallestad, a local manufacturer specializing in thermoplastic molding. Although the company was known for molding parts, it also needed mold makers. It was in that role that Treiber truly began to excel. When he wasn't working in Booker & Wallestad's toolroom, he could often be found in the workshop he'd built in the basement of his home, machining replacement parts for the company's molds. Within a few years, he decided to turn his off-hours work into an honest-to-goodness business. His new company, Custom Mold & Design, was formally established in 1965, with three employees working out of his basement.

As the years went by, Custom Mold grew out of its basement workshop and moved into more accommodating facilities in suburban New Hope. The company evolved to become a supplier specializing in high-precision molds, prototypes, and machining services for the injection molding industry. In 1986, Treiber started a sister company, Aus-Tech Mold & Design, near Austin, Texas, to meet the expanding needs of one of its biggest customers, 3M. By the time he sold the companies in 2000, he employed seventy-five people in Minnesota and Texas.

In retirement, Treiber returned to one of his earliest interests, one that predated his discovery of *Forty Power Tools You Can Make*: model making. The creative skills that helped him succeed in business served him well with each miniature ship he built. And he never forgot that he had developed many of those skills during his time at Dunwoody more than a half-century before. "That drive to create was always part of me, but I just needed a little more training," he said. "Dunwoody enabled me to become more skillful in a trade I really enjoyed. It's the best investment I ever made."

"Dunwoody enabled me to become more skillful in a trade I really enjoyed. It's the best investment I ever made."

—Duane Treiber

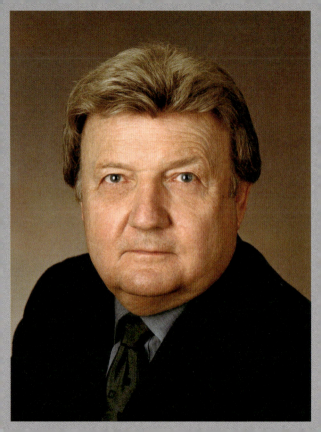

MORRIE WAGENER

Automotive Service Technology, 1957

As Morrie Wagener remembered it, he was five years old when he fell in love with cars—or, more precisely, Cords. Cord was a brand of luxury automobile manufactured in Indiana during the 1930s, and when young Wagener first laid eyes on one at a garage in his hometown of Waconia, Minnesota, he knew he was looking at something special. Over time, his fondness for Cords blossomed into an all-out love affair with fine automobiles. At age fourteen, he started working summers at a local garage, learning everything he could about cars and trucks. The more he learned, the more he realized he didn't want to spend the rest of his life on the family farm. So, he plotted an alternative. After finishing high school, he left for Minneapolis and enrolled in the Automotive program at Dunwoody Institute.

Wagener could have gone to work at any number of garages when he graduated from Dunwoody, but his fascination with luxury brands—which dated back to that first encounter with a Cord—strongly influenced his decision. In late 1957, he took a job as a mechanic at Mark Doyne's Imports on Lake Street, where he worked on MGs, Austin–Healeys, Hillmans, and other European makes. That job eventually landed him a more senior position with a startup import dealership in Wayzata. After a few years there, he bought out the owner and went into business for himself.

Morrie's Imports, as his dealership was originally known, got its first big break in 1963, when it secured a Citroën franchise. Three years later, it added Saab to its new-car mix. By the late 1960s, Morrie's had outgrown its Wayzata location. Wagener went in search of a new property, closer to downtown Minneapolis, and found one on a hillside next to Highway 12 (now I-394). When the new location of Morrie's Imports opened in 1969, it was still mainly a Saab dealership, but that soon changed. Over the next decade, it added a succession of import brands: Alfa Romeo, Lotus, Subaru, Mazda.

Morrie Wagener accepts the 2021 William and Kate Dunwoody Philanthropist Award from Dunwoody President Rich Wagner.

Wagener and his dealerships were doing well, but their long-term success was not immediately assured. During the mid-1970s, a major expansion of the Highway 12 facility strained the company's resources. A decade later, a crippling recession took a heavy toll. But Wagener, a self-described "workaholic," did not give up. "My work doesn't get any easier," he said at the time, "the numbers just get bigger." During the 1990s, the newly dubbed Morrie's Automotive Group finally started to take off. Wagener strengthened his reputation for top-notch customer service by introducing a "no hassle, no negotiation" sales approach and a "buy happy" enrollment option that offered customers free oil changes, car washes, and lifetime powertrain warranties. He also started opening new dealerships. At its height, Morrie's Automotive Group boasted fifteen dealerships in Minnesota and Wisconsin, and employed more than eight hundred people.

In 2016, after more than a half-century in the business, Wagener sold his dealerships, but the Morrie's name continued to grace the exteriors of thousands of cars sold at the locations he once owned. And like his name, his love of cars lived on. Over the years, Wagener had assembled one of the largest private classic automobile collections in the United States—including four Cords—and he kept his cars on display in a fifty-thousand-square-foot museum that reflected his disinterest in self-promotion. "Morrie's car collection is a hidden treasure," said Scott Lambert, president of the Minnesota Automobile Dealers Association. "It speaks a lot about his character that he likes to collect and restore these vehicles but doesn't have a lot of interest in showing them off."

Also speaking well of Wagener's character was his long-standing support of his alma mater. He served for many years on Dunwoody's Board of Trustees, including two as chair, and was instrumental, through his banking relationships, in helping the College weather the worldwide financial crisis of the late 2000s. He was one of the first recipients of the school's Alumni Entrepreneur Award, and in 2021, was honored with the William and Kate Dunwoody Philanthropist Award. When asked several years before that to explain his dedication to the College, his answer was unequivocal. "Without my Dunwoody education, I couldn't have figured out how all this stuff worked," he said. "But Dunwoody's mission was never just teaching technical skills. ... There has always been a big emphasis on values. I have never forgotten the lessons I learned."

"Without my Dunwoody education, I couldn't have figured out how all this stuff worked."

—Morrie Wagener

Automotive students in the "Rear Axle Section," 1920

NOEL WIEN

Automobile Repair, early 1920s

Sometime around the end of summer in 1920, a young man from Minnesota's Iron Range named Noel Wien pocketed the $700 he had recently earned through the sale of his late-model Overland touring car and set out on what he hoped would be a life-changing adventure. "I went down to Minneapolis and St. Paul to enter the William Hood Dunwoody Institute to learn about airplanes," he would later recall. Wien had never flown in a plane at that point, had never even gotten close to one, but he had become obsessed with them by reading about the exploits of pilots during World War I. He was determined to learn how to fly, and was counting on Dunwoody to teach him. There was just one problem: Dunwoody's Aeronautics program, which operated during the war, had shut down after the armistice. "Nobody there even knew where there were any airplanes or how to get to an airport," Wien said. With his flying dreams on indefinite hold, Wien developed a backup plan. He enrolled in Dunwoody's Auto Mechanics program, rented a room at a nearby boardinghouse, and kept himself fed with cheap loaves of bread purchased from the institute's Baking department.

Still, he couldn't shake his airplane obsession.

The following spring, during his second semester at Dunwoody, Wien attended an auto show, where he came across a display of a gleaming Curtiss OX-5 airplane motor. A sign next to the motor indicated that it came from the Curtiss Northwest Airplane Company, and that the company had a flying school. As soon as he could, Wien hopped a streetcar and headed out to the airfield at Snelling and Larpenteur in St. Paul, where Curtiss Northwest was headquartered. "I watched them cranking up the propellers, getting in the cockpits, running the motors up, and taking off," he recalled. "It was wonderful. All that noise!" That very day, he put his Dunwoody education on hiatus.

The adventure Wien had hoped to embark upon with his move to the Twin Cities was finally underway. After taking a series of flying lessons at Curtiss Northwest, he became a pilot with a couple local barnstorming outfits, including Federated Fliers, a flying circus founded by fellow Dunwoody alum C. W. Hinck. In 1924, he accepted an offer to fly for a startup commercial airline in Alaska. It turned out to be the beginning of a long career that would make him a legend in Alaskan aviation. As his biographer later put it, Wien became Alaska's first bush pilot, an intrepid but cautious aviator who flew "miners, adventurers, trappers, romantics, drunks, scientists, light ladies, poets, fugitives, clergymen, stowaways, madmen, prisoners, and corpses" across an area equaling "about half of Alaska." Wien's list of aviation firsts grew to include: the first flight from Anchorage to Fairbanks; the first flight and landing beyond the Arctic Circle; the first commercial flight between Fairbanks and Nome; the first passenger flight from Seattle to Fairbanks; and the first round-trip flight between North America and Asia. In 1927, he and his brother Ralph started Wien Alaska Airways, an airline that would, under various names, serve passenger and freight clients for nearly sixty years, until finally folding in 1985. His younger brother, Sig—another Dunwoody alum—would also play a critical role in the airline's success as the years went by.

Noel Wien never did finish his classes at Dunwoody after making his initial visit to Curtiss Northwest in 1921, but it's safe to assume that the training he received during his two semesters there came in handy whenever he experienced mechanical trouble in the wilds of Alaska. Like his former employer, the flying circus impresario C. W. Hinck, his Dunwoody connection features prominently on the plaque commemorating his induction into the Minnesota Aviation Hall of Fame.

In 1967, Wien Air Alaska
flew between nine Alaskan
destinations, including
Fairbanks, Nome, and Juneau.

"I went down to Minneapolis and St. Paul to enter
the William Hood Dunwoody Institute to learn
about airplanes. But when I got there, I found out
they didn't have an airplane course, just courses for
bakers, electricians, and auto mechanics."

—Noel Wien

DOUG ZUMBUSCH

Sheet Metal, 1951

Like many parents, Doug Zumbusch, owner of Dalbec Roofing in Long Lake, Minnesota, had a talent for embarrassing his kids. At least that's how his daughter, Michele Krolczyk, remembered it. "Commercial roofing is not exactly a sexy profession," she recalled. "As a kid, it was kind of embarrassing to me when he would pull a hot tar kettle behind his pickup truck, and it would be parked in our driveway, and it would stink and smell and look gross."

Zumbusch had grown up on a Buffalo, Minnesota, farm where everyone in the family was expected to pitch in. He and his wife, Bernice (a former farm kid herself), expected nothing less of their five children. "Mom and Dad were the classic middle-class couple in terms of expecting all the kids to work and pull their own weight," Krolczyk said. "It would be a cold January Saturday and my dad needed inventory done. I'd be like, 'It's freezing cold out there right now!' He'd say, 'I don't care. Get out there and count those sheets of insulation and get out and count the number of stacks of sheet metal.' And so, I did. I froze my butt off and I went out there and I did all that."

Dalbec Roofing was a family business, and always had been.

The company was founded in 1950 by Zumbusch's brother-in-law, Lester Dalbec. At about the same time Dalbec was going into business for himself, Zumbusch enrolled in the Sheet Metal program at Dunwoody Institute. Zumbusch finished his training in 1951, and soon after that, went to work for his brother-in-law, starting what would turn out to be a long career in the roofing business. Zumbusch continued to work for Dalbec until 1980, when Lester decided to retire. Doug and Bernice purchased the company and promptly moved it from its original location in Minnetonka to a new facility in nearby Long Lake.

Their daughter, Michele, was a teenager at the time, and not easily impressed, but she knew her parents were taking a big chance by taking over a business and moving it to a new location. "They took the last of their savings and bought that building in Long Lake," she said. "I can still remember their fortieth anniversary, when my sister and I brought a basket of food to them at that building. They were framing up a wall to divide the space so there was a sheet metal shop on one side and a warehouse on the other. They had gumption. And I love that they did it together."

Zumbusch's kids were also very aware that their father took great pride in his Dunwoody education. He was the only member of his family to attend an institution of higher learning, and his children made him smile by declaring, "There's where Dad went to school!" almost every time they passed the Dunwoody campus on their drives into the City from their home in the western suburbs.

Doug and Bernice ran Dalbec Roofing for another fifteen years before deciding that they, too, were ready for retirement. By then, the company was bringing in about $2 million a year in revenue. They sold Dalbec to Michele and her husband, effectively keeping the business in the family. The company took a new name, Mint Roofing, and continued to grow. In 2016, Michele accepted an invitation to deliver the keynote address at the College's annual Kate Dunwoody Society Luncheon. That experience led her to get more deeply involved with the College by, among other things, volunteering to sit on the Alumni Association Board. "It felt a little odd because I didn't actually graduate from Dunwoody," she said. "So, I sit in place of my father—at least that's how I put it."

Bernice and Doug Zumbusch purchased Dalbec Roofing from Doug's brother-in-law, Lester Dalbec, in 1980.

"They were framing up a wall to divide the space so there was a sheet metal shop on one side and a warehouse on the other. They had gumption. And I love that they did it together."

—Michele Krolczyk on her parents, Doug and Bernice Zumbusch

CONCLUSION

Scott Stallman, Ph.D.
President, Dunwoody College of Technology (2024–)

Dunwoody is a special place, with a culture of innovation, curiosity, and commitment you don't find at other colleges. It was something I recognized when I first started here more than three years ago. It continues to be the primary reason I intend to retire from Dunwoody. There is no better college to work for, or to enroll in.

I've been in higher education for more than two decades. I've spent many of those years at other community and technical colleges. On the surface, they may share a similar purpose, but when you look a little deeper—to the people behind the Dunwoody story—there is simply no comparison.

The graduates who are highlighted within the pages of this book have come from different backgrounds, they have chosen different fields, and walked different paths. But they share a common thread. They share a spirit of innovation, creativity, and entrepreneurship.

Those traits are embedded in the Dunwoody culture, fostered by the faculty and staff, and embodied in our students. Students who will contribute to the next generation of success stories.

The Dunwoody legacy has been built by those who came before us. These people shaped industries, built businesses, and drove solutions. It's because of their accomplishments that the Dunwoody story will live on and thrive into an ever-changing and dynamic future.

One of the things that makes Dunwoody so unique in the field of technical and skilled trade education is we're not just training people to do a job—we're teaching them to solve problems. Recent graduates and future students will be solving tomorrow's challenges—in the areas of green energy, cybersecurity, advanced manufacturing, and Industry 4.0.

I'm consistently inspired and impressed by our alumni, who work to make the world a better place, to find solutions and contribute to their communities and their industries.

The world needs more problem solvers, and Dunwoody will continue to be a place where the curious and creative can discover their talents and hone their skills.

I'm excited to read the next chapter of the Dunwoody legacy and the stories that will shape our future.

ACKNOWLEDGMENTS

Dunwoody College of Technology would like to extend a special thank you to Ray Newkirk '65, Machine Tool Technology, Honorary Trustee. This work was made possible because of his vision, leadership, and support.

We are also grateful for the many Dunwoody alumni, friends, and family who allowed us to share their stories within the pages of this book. Their stories reflect the "Born To *Do*" spirit and serve as an inspiration for future generations of Dunwoody students.

Lastly, we would like to thank the Dunwoody Institutional Advancement and Marketing departments, along with the editorial team, for their work throughout this book building process.

IMAGE CREDITS

Alaska State Library
254

ArieStudio – stock.adobe.com
90

Ascension Catholic School
153

AVID International
Molding Solutions
162

Steve Cukrov – stock.adobe.com
72

Dunwoody College of
Technology
ii, v, 6, 7 (3), 8 (3), 9 (3), 10, 14,
22–23, 24, 27, 28, 31, 40–41,
46, 49, 54, 64, 70, 74–75, 80,
84, 86, 100–101, 110–111,
112, 120–121, 132, 150,
154–155, 168, 172, 180, 188,
192–193, 196, 198–199, 200,
203, 212–213, 222, 230–231,
232, 240, 244, 250, 252–253,
266

JaCiva's Bakery
62

Konrad Marine
141

M. A. Mortenson Company
164, 166

Metal Craft
171

Minnesota Historical Society
36, 57, 76, 116, 142, 156, 208,
214, 226

Northland Concrete & Masonry
206

Polaris Industries
106, 109

RPC
238

Courtesy Greg Arvig
18, 20

Courtesy John Cleveland
32

Courtesy Harvey and Joyce Dahl
42, 45

Courtesy Paul Davis
50

Courtesy Joel Elftmann
58

Courtesy Jill Englund
66, 69

Courtesy Tom Gauthier
88

Courtesy Mike Hanson
96, 99

Courtesy Jim Hentschell
102

Courtesy Gary Janisch
122

Courtesy Mark Jessen
126, 129

Courtesy Jay Johnson
130

Courtesy Ken Konrad
138

Courtesy Michele Krolczyk
258, 261

Courtesy Austin Lutz
146, 149

Courtesy Cory and Collin Miller
160

Courtesy Ray Newkirk
174

Courtesy Dale Nordquist
176, 178

Courtesy Bob Porter
184, 186

Courtesy Larry Raasch
194

Courtesy Sarah Richards
134

Courtesy Doug Schieffer
204

Courtesy Anthony Scott
92

Courtesy Mark Sherry
218

Courtesy Steve Stone
234

Courtesy Vern Taaffe
236

Courtesy Morrie Wagener
248

Dave Kenney Collection
16, 38, 124